W9-CZU-595

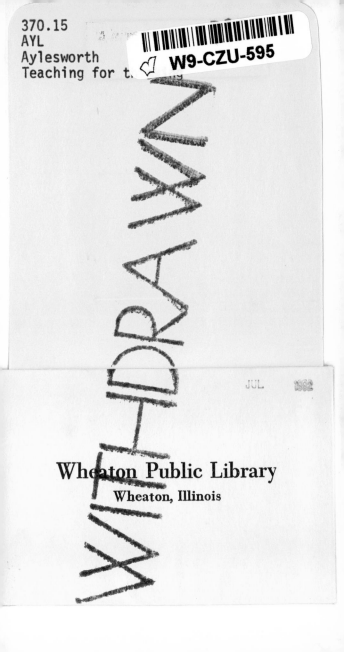

TEACHING FOR THINKING

DR. THOMAS G. AYLESWORTH is a Senior Editor for a major publisher and was previously Senior Editor of *Current Science*. He is the author of four books: *Planning for Effective Science Teaching, Our Polluted World, This Vital Air—This Vital Water,* and *It Works Like This*. His other writings include numerous articles for professional journals. His extensive teaching experience includes junior and senior high school science, and science education classes on the elementary and secondary levels to both graduate and undergraduate students at Michigan State University. He has also conducted science-education workshops and has taught graduate classes for Wesleyan University.

DR. GERALD M. REAGAN, an Associate Professor at the Ohio State University, holds the A.B. degree from the University of Nebraska, the M.A. from Western Michigan University, and the Ph.D. from Michigan State University. He has taught history at the junior and senior high school level, and the Philosophy of Education and Foundations of Education at Michigan State University, University of Tennessee, the University of California at Los Angeles, and Syracuse University.

TEACHING FOR THINKING

Thomas G. Aylesworth
AND
Gerald M. Reagan

GARDEN CITY, NEW YORK
Doubleday & Company, Inc.
1969

Grateful acknowledgment is made to Harper & Row, Publishers, for permission to quote from *The Adventures of Huckleberry Finn* by Mark Twain.

Material is also quoted from the following books, published by Doubleday & Company, Inc.: *Follow Me, Everybody* by Craig Bettinger, copyright © 1968 by Doubleday & Company, Inc.; *The Miracle of Flight* by Richard Cromer, copyright © 1968 by Don Meier Productions, Inc.; *The Game* by Richard E. Drdek, copyright © 1968 by Richard E. Drdek; *Koalas Live Here* by Irmengarde Eberle, copyright © 1967 by Irmengarde Eberle Koehler; *The Riddle of the Red Whale* by Edward Fenton, copyright © 1966 by Edward Fenton; *Discovering Rocks and Minerals* by Roy A. Gallant and Christopher Schuberth, copyright © 1967 by Doubleday & Company, Inc.; *Jim Starling and the Colonel* by E. Wallace Hildick, copyright © 1960 by E. W. Hildick; *Jill and the Applebird House* by Ruth Holberg, copyright © 1968 by Ruth Langland Holberg; *The Cow That Spoke for Seppl* by Robert E. Huldschiner, copyright © 1968 by Doubleday & Company, Inc.; *Leaders of New Nations* by Leonard S. Kenworthy and Erma Farrari, copyright © 1959, 1968 by Doubleday & Company, Inc.; *Crystals of Life: The Story of Salt* by Robert Kraske, copyright © 1968 by Robert Kraske; *The Impossibles* by Agnes McCarthy, copyright © 1968 by Agnes McCarthy; *Room 10* by Agnes McCarthy, copyright © 1966 by Agnes McCarthy; *Images of the Universe* by Richard McLanathan, copyright © 1966 by Richard McLanathan; *Clocks, Calendars and Carrousels* by John G. Navarra, copyright © 1967 by John G. Navarra; *For Pepita—An Orange Tree* by Claire Oleson, copyright © 1967 by Doubleday & Company, Inc.; *Words Words Words* by Mary O'Neill, copyright © 1966 by Mary O'Neill; *The Fantastic Breed* by Leon Phillips, copyright © 1968 by Doubleday & Company, Inc.; *Probability: The Science of Chance* by Arthur G. Razzell and K. G. O. Watts, copyright © 1964, 1967 by Arthur G. Razzell and K. G. O. Watts; *The Hopefuls* by Lloyd Robinson, copyright © 1966 by Doubleday & Company, Inc.; *The Stolen Election* by Lloyd Robinson, copyright © 1968 by Doubleday & Company, Inc.; *Two for Trouble* by Eileen Rosenbaum, copyright © 1967 by Eileen Rosenbaum; *Veronica Ganz* by Marilyn Sachs, copyright © 1968 by Marilyn Sachs; *Masters of Music* by Dorothy and Joseph Samachson, copyright © 1967 by Dorothy Samachson and Joseph Samachson; *Clean Air—Sparkling Water* by Dorothy E. Shuttlesworth, copyright © 1968 by Dorothy E. Shuttlesworth; *Four Took Freedom* by Phillip Sterling and Rayford Logan, copyright © 1967 by Doubleday & Company, Inc.; and *Hide-Out for a Horse* by Gerry Turner, copyright © 1967 by Gerry Turner.

For John S. Richardson
scholar, teacher, friend

CONTENTS

TEACHING FOR THINKING

Critical Thinking as a Skill

There is a strong possibility that the skill subjects are the most effectively taught curricular areas in the American public schools. Music, fine and related arts, typing, driver education, shorthand, and physical education seem to make more lasting impressions on students than do science, social studies, mathematics, and the language arts. When adults review memories of their educational experiences, they tend to talk of their experiences in the band or chorus, or the football or basketball team—seldom do they mention the happy times they had in social studies or mathematics. When they put into practice some of the things they were taught in school during their leisure hours, they tend to drive, to paint, to work in a woodshop, to cook exotic dishes—seldom do they solve complicated geometry problems or dissect a frog. When they utilize school learnings in their professional lives, they tend to type, to take shorthand, or to construct objects—seldom do they read a book, write a theme, or hold a spelling bee.

Perhaps we can account for the apparent differences in permanence of learning, usefulness of the content area, and enjoyment of education between the "practical" skill subjects and the "abstract" academic subjects by pointing out that teachers of skill subjects generally encourage students to behave as practitioners rather than observers, while teachers of academic subjects, on the other hand, tend to neglect teaching meaningful skills as integral parts of subject matter.

Attention needs to be paid to the two more prominent types of skills in the classroom: manipulative and cognitive. Manipulative skill is concerned with the ability to handle data or things in an immediate and largely repetitive way; whereas cognitive skill is concerned with the ability to handle data and things through processes underlying wholly manipulative skills—i.e., principles, hypotheses, and understandings which would allow one to explain manipulative skill and its relevance to a particular situation. Teachers in self-contained classrooms, judging by their actions in most situations, use two separate approaches to teaching: skill and academic. If teachers can eliminate this dichotomy, learners will profit more from their education.

THE LEARNER AS PRACTITIONER

When the learner first begins to study music or art, he begins to practice the skills of the musician or the artist. The same holds true in all skill subjects; that is, he is encouraged immediately to develop the skills of the practitioner of the subject. In driver-education class, he drives; in woodshop, he uses tools; in typing class, he types. He is, from the first day of school, behaving as an artist, a musician, or a driver. The teacher emphasizes professional skills and authentic behavior. The learner is permitted to make mistakes and profit from his errors.

On the other hand, seldom does the science learner discover anything that is new to the world of science—though it may be new to him personally; seldom does the social-studies learner synthesize various political and historical points of view; seldom does the mathematics learner apply mathematics to real-life situations; and seldom does the language-arts learner behave as a literary critic. All of these skills are predigested by the teacher.

After a period of time in skill practice, the art learner studies paint-mixing, the music learner studies harmony and counterpoint, the typing learner studies business-letter style, the woodshop learner studies drafting, and the physical-education learner studies football plays. Essentially, however, in the skill subjects, acquisition of skills precedes acquisition of knowledge; practical, concrete matters come before academic, abstract matters. Therefore, the learner is first a practitioner and next a student. Thus, if art is a vocational subject for him, his first understandings are of art as a practitioner. If it is a nonvocational subject, he at least understands how artists work. No wonder we find more appreciations of the skill subjects in our adult population.

In the academic subjects the situation is reversed. The skills of science are postponed until the students acquire what is fondly called the "tools" of science: a large vocabulary and an understanding of the discoveries of the past. He is not encouraged to practice mathematical, social, or language skills until he has had a thorough grounding in the history of the subject area. He is not encouraged to derive formulae, formulate historical hypotheses, or make speeches until he learns about the formulae, hypotheses, and speeches of the past.

In short, the learner must first be a student and then a practitioner. Most people never reach the point of becoming practitioners in the academic subjects; they thus build up stereotypes of the scientist and mathematician as stuffy, hyperintelligent, sexless persons, and the writer and historian as effeminate, bookish, otherworldly persons. Few adults understand the academicians, because they have never practiced the arts of the academicians. While they may understand the technicians in the academic fields, they look upon the theoreticians as eggheads.

A skill most often overlooked by teachers of the academic subjects is that of critical thinking: that is, the mental skill of solving problems in the manner of the practitioner. Critical thinking is the lifework of the academicians, and learners are rarely given the opportunity to behave in this manner. In spite of protestations to the contrary, the schools tend to teach *what* to think rather than *how* to think. If an attempt to teach how to think is made, it is often at an ill-defined or even unconscious level. When students are taught how to think properly, they are also able to learn what to think, since limits are automatically set to the kinds of evidence that are acceptable and the methods of thinking procedure that are allowed. The learner who lacks explicit knowledge of the structure of academic work, furthermore, having an increased amount of leisure time, will have an opportunity to wreak social havoc because of his lack of analytical and synthetic skill.

In the following example from a biology class in a high school, the students were to begin a laboratory dissection of the frog. By nature, we would assume that the laboratory situation would lend itself to an experience in critical thinking.

TEACHER: We'll start our dissection of the frog, and I wish that all of you would make a determined effort to learn and know these things that we are trying to present. Today, particularly, we will be looking for different structures in the mouth of the frog, and we will be starting into the internal structures as well. We'll look at some muscle structures in the hind leg of the frog, finding out how the legs operate. I'm going to pass around to you a piece of paper on which you will immediately put the names of both laboratory partners. Choose a partner. I think in most cases the people at the table you're sitting at will be sufficient, but in a few cases we'll allow some changing around. You will find on page 361 the picture of the frog with the various organs listed. If you will make a list of those organs on your piece of paper, and as you remove them from the frog be sure to lay the organ that you remove with the name upon the paper. Now I'll keep moving around the class, and as you get the right organ with the proper name I'll sign that particular thing, and when you get through this list of names of organs with my name on each one, it will be a basis for grading on dissection. So you'll retain this paper for about two days.

STUDENT: Did you hear about the boy in the other class? They gave him a dollar to eat a frog eyeball.

TEACHER: O. K.

STUDENT: You're dripping all over my paper.

TEACHER: You don't have to put them in any particular position. Take one hind leg and cut around the base of the leg. There. This loose skin here—start cutting and keep the scissors pointed just beneath the skin. That skin will come right off like pulling a long glove off or a sock. Turn it inside out and pull it right off the leg. I've soaked these to get the formaldehyde off so it won't smell so bad. Pull the skin right off so it will reveal the muscles. Pull it back and keep on. It will come off if you pull hard enough. Now, let's move on with this. Some of you people will be behind us. This is what I want you to do now. You'll notice the muscles of the leg. Now, this particular joint compares with our heel, and this one here compares with our knee. What I'd like you to do is—the muscle that is attached between the knee and the heel is large. It lies there loose from all the other muscles; in fact, it's loose from itself except at each point. If you'll cut that muscle at the knee, it will hang loose from the bone. Then we can show you how that leg operates. You will see that groove in the joint through which the tendon runs. It runs through that groove in the joint like a rope in a pulley. Here's the way that operates. A muscle only operates by contraction and cannot extend itself. It has to be extended by another muscle that is operating just opposing it. And it would be this small muscle on this side of the leg. Now, if you want to cut that one free, too, you'll find that this one is more closely connected to the bone. The smaller one on the front, where the shin is. Now the reason that we cut them free is that these muscles have set up what we call *rigor mortis*. They are rigid and we are going to try to duplicate their action. The leg is straightened by pulling on this muscle, which stimulates the action of that muscle when it contracts, so that when the frog jumps, this muscle contracts, straightening out this leg. See that? See the action of that?

This laboratory period could have been utilized to give the learners a stimulating experience in critical thinking, in finding out for themselves, or in operating as scientists. Instead, it became a teacher-dominated, boring period of following directions. Students were not permitted to explore, to ask questions, or to formulate hypotheses. The interest level was low, as can be seen when considering the students' statements. Essentially, this laboratory period was little more than a class lecture. This exercise in teacher-dominated fact-finding is not an example of searching for truth through critical thinking, but upon completion of the lesson the teacher held the opinion that it was a period of exploration and problem-solving. Perhaps some operational definitions are called for.

THE TYPES OF THINKING

Most anthropologists today would probably agree with Linton that

. . . from the physical point of view, man is merely another large terrestrial primate. . . . He is set off from the other members of his order, and indeed from other mammals in general, by his tremendous ability to learn, to think, and to communicate to others what he has learned and thought.[1]

Inasmuch as learning and communicating are based upon thinking, perhaps it is this last-named ability that truly sets man apart from other animals. Granting that many persons hold that other animals can think in a primitive way, abstract reasoning is a capability with which only man is endowed. Despite all the publicity given to talking dogs and horses that can add numbers, man remains the only animal that depends not upon

[1] Ralph Linton, *The Tree of Culture* (New York: Alfred A. Knopf, 1955), p. 7.

his instincts but upon his brain—he is the only animal that can devise alternatives. Each time he comes to a choice between two or more courses of action, he is confronted by a problem that must be solved. He solves these problems in one of four basic ways, or using one of four methods.

The persistency process. The first, and lowest in the hierarchy, may be called the persistency process. By using this method we solve a problem in a certain manner simply because we have always solved this problem in this manner. For example, many people have fallen into the habit of buying the same make of automobile each time they trade in their old car, although they obviously have several other choices. Why? Because they have always purchased this brand. In elections, many citizens vote not for the man but for the party, simply because it is a habit with them.

How can we use this method in the classroom? We try to teach learners to keep the room clean, to put away their equipment, and do countless tasks of this nature simply because they have always done so. This type of problem-solving borders on the conditioned response, but it is also the utilization of the persistency process.

The testimonial process. The second type of thinking, or problem-solving, is the testimonial process. In this method we solve problems in a given way because someone of consequence or status has dictated that we take a certain course of action, or we read an answer to a question in a book. Many people eat a given type of breakfast food merely because a baseball player has told them to do so in an advertisement. In elections, some citizens vote for a candidate because they are convinced by a newspaper which supports him.

In the classroom it would be rather difficult to teach a concept such as the effects of outer space on our bodies, without getting most of the information from reading or interviewing. Obviously, also, most of the biographical material about great men and women must be obtained vicariously, generally through the testimonial process.

The innate process. The third method, and the most maligned one, is the innate process, sometimes called intuitive or instinctive reasoning. Some persons use this method to pick racehorses, others to pick presidential candidates, but the process is placed third on the list because there is a great deal of previous experience involved in selecting answers to questions through this method.

In the classroom, we hope to teach some social values through this procedure. Learners, for example, do not say "please" and "thank you" because some authority has told them to, nor do they do so because they have always done it. Any parent can vouch for this. If they demonstrate social skills, we hope it is because they have innately reasoned that other people should be treated with respect. We want learners to acquire social grace on the innate level.

Critical thinking. The final, most complex method of problem-solving is the method called critical thinking. John Dewey outlined this age-old procedure in a series of steps: (1) identify the problem, (2) establish facts, (3) formulate hypotheses, (4) test hypotheses, and (5) evaluate results.[2] When we budget our paychecks, we are forced to use this method in order to choose those expenditures that are necessary and do

---

[2] John Dewey, *How We Think* (Boston: D. C. Heath, 1933), p. 292.

not exceed our salaries. When a student carries out his own experiments to a conclusion, he is forced to use this method in order to solve his original problem effectively. The method of critical thinking is often called the most intellectual of all methods because it is the only one of the four that can possibly admit to an error, inasmuch as testing hypotheses is not a part of the other three.

It is extremely important that we teach learners to derive facts, concepts, and principles through the use of this procedure. The first reason for this desirability is that many of the learners' important decisions during the rest of their lives cannot be derived satisfactorily in any other way. Too many people select candidates, budget money, and pick wives and husbands through the use of the persistency, testimonial, and innate processes.

Secondly, learners must be taught to use critical thinking, because there are many people in this country who are constantly attempting to prevent their using it. We want our pupils to be able to pierce through the arguments that capitalize on established habits, the voice of authority, or appeals to emotion, and arrive at conclusions that are scientific.

The third reason for helping learners to use critical thinking is that they will not necessarily improve in their ability to solve problems scientifically as they grow older. It is a skill, and thus must be practiced under the guidance of a teacher.

ANALYTICAL AND SYNTHETIC THINKING

Inasmuch as the intellectual attitude which regards all questions as proper and all answers as tentative is intertwined with the ability to think critically, attention must be paid to both types of reasoning procedures—analytical and synthetic reasoning. These are the two faces of critical thinking, and learners as citizens have need for both abilities, depending upon what types of problems must be solved.

Analytical thinking (sometimes called *deductive reasoning*) is that type of problem-solving that leads from the general to the particular, from the universal to the individual, from conclusion to premise—in short, from principle to facts. Synthetic thinking (sometimes called *inductive reasoning*), on the other hand, leads from the particular to the general, from the individual to the universal, from premise to conclusion, or from facts to principle. It would appear, as will be discussed later, that analytical thinking is most often used by persons engaged in thinking critically in the areas of mathematics and language arts, while synthetic thinking is most appropriate in the areas of science and social studies. Thus, both are extremely important in the preparation of thinking citizens.

There is an implication in the foregoing paragraphs that the analytical and synthetic methods of thinking are discrete entities. This would be an incorrect assumption because, since man is a creature of experience, pure analytical thinking is impossible; man's experience is never complete enough to permit this method of problem-solving. He could never know all of the principles governing the facts he is seeking; therefore, he must become acquainted with additional principles through the use of synthetic reasoning. Also, pure synthetic reasoning is impossible, since man must always solve problems by relating them to past experience. He will rarely be concerned with a group of facts about which he knows no principles. In short, most of man's critical-thinking activities are combinations of analytical and synthetic thinking.

THE STATUS OF CRITICAL THINKING IN THE CLASSROOM

It has been concluded many times, both descriptively and experimentally, that there is a lack of direct teaching of critical thinking in our schools, that students need practice in critical thinking in order to utilize the method effectively, and that teachers approve of this method in theory but not in practice. Thus, it would seem highly desirable that steps be taken to help teachers to relate their theoretical belief in critical thinking to the practical application of teaching this method directly in the classroom.

The importance of giving practice in critical thinking to the learners in the classroom has been developed in studies that demonstrate that a knowledge of facts does not necessarily lead to an application of these facts; that there may be little relationship between intelligence and reasoning ability or between age and reasoning ability; and, furthermore, that there is no corresponding development in reasoning ability as the learner grows older. On the other hand, while factual knowledge may aid in the explanation of phenomena, it was found that the ability to think critically aids the student in all types of reasoning situations.

There would seem to be little disagreement among the research people in this area of education that practice in critical thinking is necessary in the curriculum of the school. Most of these people deplore the lack of this type of teaching, and most of them point out or imply that we are cheating school children, and consequently future generations, by not effectively equipping learners to think critically.

It is not enough merely to discuss critical thinking in order to enable children to exhibit a scientific attitude to such a degree that they will utilize the method of critical thinking, not only in the classroom, but also in their daily lives. Learners must have practice in using this procedure, and this can only come about through the teacher's purposeful planning. The teacher must provide opportunities for the students to utilize the method. Many opportunities for this direct teaching of critical thinking arise daily.

For fifty years, teachers have been urged to utilize critical thinking in the classroom as a way in which to equip learners to cope with the world. Apparently, this has not been done, since author after author decries the fact that problem-solving methodology, with emphasis on critical thinking, is not found in the classroom. In summarizing the results and conclusions of research in the area of teaching learners to think critically, several generalizations seem to be evident that indicate not only the desirability of the teaching of critical thinking, but also the need for this type of teaching.

THE ROLE OF THE TEACHER

When a child asks a legitimate question for which he desires an answer, he has identified a problem. It is the role of the teacher, then, to assist him in the establishment of facts, formulation of hypotheses, testing of hypotheses, and evaluation of results. Rather than answer a question of importance directly, therefore, the teacher should help the child find sources of information, develop possible answers, set up experiments and demonstrations, and help in any other way with the solution to the problem. The solution, however, should come from the learner. All too often, the teacher gives way to the temptation of answering the question directly, and thus forces the child to solve his problem by using the testimonial process, an appeal to the voice of authority.

Certainly not all learners will be able to identify problems with the same degree of efficiency, and in many cases it will become the teacher's responsibility to suggest problems for the learners. In this way, the method of asking questions, provided that the questions are of real significance to the learner, becomes a method of assisting learners to identify problems.

Once a problem is identified, the teacher can elicit possible hypotheses from the child or children, but he must be prepared to help the learners formulate these hypotheses. Through all of the steps, the teacher must be ready to give help, but he must be hesitant about supplying too much information. This would stand in the way of the learners' learning to think critically on their own.

Of course, if the pupils suggest a method of testing a hypothesis that appears to be too dangerous, or too expensive, or too time-consuming, the teacher must veto the suggestion. The teacher is the leader of the group and has the responsibility to see that learners develop principles with maximum efficiency.

Critical thinking is not a fixed set of steps, however. While it is rare that a step can be eliminated, the sequence of steps may be modified. We find ourselves many times every day drawing a conclusion, only to have the original problem change. For example, in planning a budget, we may conclude that we can buy some luxury, only to discover a new bill in the mail. We may decide that we can cross the street, only to have the traffic light change. On a higher level, when Alexander Fleming discovered the effects of penicillin, he was confronted by a conclusion, and was forced to derive a problem from a conclusion. But from the ability to think critically comes flexibility, and from flexibility comes maturity—the ability to foresee consequences and to abide by the results of our actions.

Let us investigate an actual example of a teacher working with a pupil in the second grade. The child had a block of wood, eight inches by eight inches by one inch. He also had a length of dowel rod, a nail, and a small flag. He stated the problem to the teacher: "I want to find the center of this block of wood so that I can pound the nail up through it into this rod and make a flagpole out of it."

The teacher asked him if his knowledge of the straight-edge rule would help him with this, and he replied, "I think so."

In testing his hypothesis ("I'll measure halfway across the top and halfway down the side.") he derived a tentative operational definition of the concept "center," but he made a miscalculation and the block looked like this:

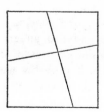

The teacher directed him to look at the block to see what had happened, and he saw that the lines did not emerge in the proper places. He then evolved the hypothesis, "The middles of all four sides should be used." The result was:

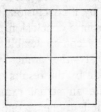

Many teachers would have stopped at this point, but this boy's teacher raised another problem: "Could you find the center of the board by using only a straight stick?"

She helped him see the relationships between diagonal corners and the center of a square figure, and he had this result:

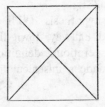

This boy had solved a geometry problem with his teacher's help. He had had an experience of importance to him, and since it was of importance and he had done it himself, it probably was remembered for a much longer period of time than might otherwise be expected.

In conclusion, direct teaching of critical thinking permits learners to behave as practitioners behave—they are not merely acting as reviewers or spectators, checking over what has been read in a book or explained by the teacher. Thousands of people in this country (for example, many in politics and advertising) earn their living by attempting to make people solve problems by using the persistency process, the testimonial process, or the innate process. Learners must be helped to use critical thinking or they will be enslaved by their education, not freed.

Learning to read exposes the reader indiscriminately to the best and the worst—the statesman and the demagogue, the physician and the quack. A new literacy in critical analysis is required, so that the learner can become responsible and can force those who are irresponsible in the marketplace of ideas either to become responsible or find out that no one will buy their wares.

The Practitioner's Use of the Synthetic Skill

Before we can make an analysis of the work of the social scientist or the natural scientist, we need to set up at least one ground rule—that of position, job, or occupation. In short, we need a definition of the way in which they earn a living.

There are relatively few social or natural scientists who can earn a living in the social or natural sciences exclusively. They are, therefore, required to become occupational schizophrenics. They must teach school at the same time that they carry on their research. This means that we must separate in our minds that part of their daily work in which they communicate with learners from that part of their daily work in which they communicate with their colleagues. So let us forget, for the time being, that most social and natural scientists are teachers.

AN EXAMPLE FROM NATURAL SCIENCE

In order to show how natural scientists go about their research, let us take a case in point: the synthesis of virus from inert chemicals. This was a discovery made independently by two groups of men.

Dr. George W. Cochran and a group of virologists at Utah State University, and a team at the University of California at Los Angeles—Dr. Sam G. Wildman and Dr. Young Tai Kim—performed the investigations. Knowing, in general, the chemical make-up of the typical virus, they set about to manufacture these viruses.

They found that when the nucleic acid part of the core of the tobacco mosaic virus was injected into a test tube containing inert chemicals, the nucleic acid synthesized new viruses—protein and all—from the non-living chemicals. In essence, this was the creation of life in a test tube.

What elements of the critical thinking process are found here? The first step, isolating the problem, is here. The problem probably went something like this: "How can viruses be synthesized from inert chemicals?" Many hypotheses undoubtedly went through their minds, but the one in which the test was successful was: "The nucleic acid core of the tobacco mosaic virus will synthesize protein molecules which, with the acid, will form new viruses."

The test for this hypothesis was to do the proposed experiment. The conclusion that was drawn confirmed the hypothesis, and we seem to find ourselves on the brink of a discovery in the study of the formation of life. This much is an example of how a scientist uses the method of critical thinking.

AN EXAMPLE FROM THE SOCIAL SCIENCES

Many years ago, Dr. Margaret Mead, the anthropologist, made a trip to the Admiralty Islands in order to study the Manu culture. At that time, the Admiralties were quite backward, and Dr. Mead returned home with a great deal of descriptive material about these primitive people. So far, this is not really a synthesis of information, except in the most gross form. It is, rather, a descriptive essay.

World War II came and went, and the Manus changed. They had been half-civilized by their contact with soldiers, sailors, and marines, and had changed their way of life to a great extent. Dr. Mead returned and gathered more data about them and the changes that had occurred in their way of life.

This time a synthesis came out of the investigation. World War II caused certain effects on their civilization. Now Dr. Mead had a comparative study.

Her problem might have been: "In what way did World War II have a civilizing influence on the Manus of the Admiralty Islands?" Her hypothesis could have been: "Many of the more primitive practices of these people will have disappeared." Her method of testing the hypothesis was to make another trip to gather data, and her conclusion was a confirmation of the hypothesis.

WHAT DID THEY DO?

Essentially, these two studies in the natural and social sciences performed the same function: They resulted in the formation of a new principle. In one, life can be created by man. In the other, contact with civilized people tends to civilize primitive cultures. Both of these studies were examples of the synthetic function of critical thinking. They both represent the finding of a generalization.

Another similarity between the two studies was the presence of a control. In one, it was a vast number of trials in which a statistically valid number of samples produced the same result. In the other, the control was the previous study—the "before" picture—with which the later study was compared.

Another similarity was that both of the studies were presented to the world in the same way. They were discussed at professional meetings and were written up in the professional literature.

Almost all research and discovery carried on in either the natural or the social sciences is of the synthetic variety. That is, a new principle, generalization, or fact is discovered that came from previously known items of information.

A STUMBLING BLOCK

A note of warning should be sounded at this point. There are times when the natural or social scientist forgets that he is a synthesizer and tries to become an analyzer. That is, he takes the principle that he has formed and tries to work backwards toward a fact, or a subprinciple. Thus, we find the unhappy situation where some natural scientists have told the press that we are now in a position to eradicate all viruses, since we know so much about them. Here they were trying to take the new principle, that we can create virus life, and work back to an individual case, that we can eliminate these microorganisms. This statement in the press reflects a profound lack of understanding of the ecological balance of nature.

Also, if Dr. Mead were to make some startling pronouncements about the influences of civilization on individual Manus, she would be overstepping the bounds of synthesis into analysis. She did not make this mistake, but not every social-science investigator is able to resist this temptation.

It may very well be that those practitioners who are used to the synthetic method find it hard to use the analytical method, and vice versa. This would tend to explain some of the nonsense that supposedly educated people pass off as truth from time to time. They are trying to communicate in an area outside their field by using an unfamiliar technique.

AN EXAMPLE FROM A SCIENCE CLASS

STUDENT: When we studied about chemical and physical changes we found out that rust is a chemical change. Does that mean that, in the end, rust cannot be prevented? Not even by painting the iron or steel?

TEACHER: Do cars and other newly painted iron and steel surfaces rust?

STUDENT: No, not right away. But they often start to rust after a year or two.

TEACHER: What prevents rust in that first year?

STUDENT: New paint.

TEACHER: Then, doesn't paint prevent rust, at least for a while?

STUDENT: Yes, but how can we make it last longer?

STUDENT: You could put it on thicker.

STUDENT: You could put it on every two years or so. Bridges and highway signs get painted every five years or so to keep them from rusting away.

STUDENT: But they still get some rust. How can we invent a paint that will keep iron from rusting for fifty years? You can't do it by putting paint on thicker,

and even when you paint every two years, some rust
gets in there.

STUDENT: Rust is a chemical change. You can't stop it.
Iron just gets rusty. I don't think you can make a
paint that will last a long time.

TEACHER: What is necessary for the chemical change to
occur?

STUDENT: Oxygen unites with the iron surface and forms
iron oxide. The iron itself changes when air can
get to it.

STUDENT: If we could keep the air from getting to the iron,
this iron oxide would not form. Paint keeps the
oxygen away from the iron.

TEACHER: Does this fact mean that we can find a rustproofing paint?

STUDENT: Yes, if we could find a paint that prevents the
oxygen and iron or steel from uniting in the form
of rust.

TEACHER: Does anyone know of such a paint?

STUDENT: No, but aren't some better than others?

STUDENT: Can we find out?

TEACHER: How?

STUDENT: Let's all find all the different kinds of paint that
we can and paint nails. Then we can submerge
them in water and . . .

In this case, the problem was: "Will paint protect
an iron or steel surface from rust?" The hypothesis was
that paint would. The students were then going to test
this hypothesis by using many different kinds of paint.
You should notice that the teacher kept in the back-
ground, for the most part, only entering the conversation when some direction was needed.

AN EXAMPLE FROM A SOCIAL STUDIES CLASS

TEACHER: What things go into making up the democratic way of life?

STUDENT: Good people.

STUDENT: What do you mean by good people?

STUDENT: People who go to school.

TEACHER: Do all people who go to school turn out to be good citizens?

STUDENT: No, but I think we can agree that they are on the right road to being good citizens.

STUDENT: Elections are important, too.

STUDENT: I don't think they are necessary.

STUDENT: But you have to elect officers so that the different branches of government can be filled.

STUDENT: That sounds good, but couldn't we get this job done just as well without elections?

STUDENT: I don't know.

STUDENT: Why couldn't the officers be just picked without an election?

STUDENT: How would you like it if your mother told you what to spend your allowance on, or if the teachers picked class officers?

STUDENT: It's not fair to do things that way.

STUDENT: Maybe it is—maybe it isn't. Let's try it.

STUDENT: How?

STUDENT: Mr. X [indicating teacher], could you run this class in an undemocratic way for a few days?

TEACHER: I think so.

STUDENT: Then we'll find out the difference.

Here the problem was: "What is an undemocratic society like?" The hypothesis expressed by a majority of the learners was that they would not be likely to enjoy it. Although they conceived of an undemocratic situation as being primarily authoritarian, and while the teacher may not be able to play the role of dictator effectively, the class is well on its way toward testing the hypothesis. Notice that the original impetus—the statement of the problem—was made by the teacher. It would appear, however, that the students were reacting positively toward the idea.

In these examples, the students were synthesizing. They were arriving at, or attempting to arrive at, a principle. In one case, small bits of information were being marshaled to prove a generalization about paint and rust. In the other, we find a generalization about authoritarianism and justice. Both classes were behaving as practitioners.

The Practitioner's Use of the Analytical Skill

Those who use the analytical skill, like those who use the synthetic skill, are usually teachers. They may be mathematicians, writers, or speechmakers. However, most often they are also educators. Once again, we must separate that part of their positions—the teaching part—that involves appreciations, from that part of their positions—the mathematician, writer, or speaker part—that involves discovery.

AN EXAMPLE FROM MATHEMATICS

When Pythagoras developed his theorem, he concluded with something akin to our equation $a^2 = b^2 + c^2$—that is, that the square of the hypotenuse of a right triangle is equal to the sum of the squares of the other two sides.

His mental processes of critical thinking may have gone like this. The problem was: "Is there a relationship between the two sides of a right triangle and the hypotenuse?" The hypotenuse was an agreement, the testing of the hypothesis was mental or written, and the conclusion confirmed the hypothesis.

The difference between this discovery and the discovery of the creation of viruses was that Pythagoras was using the analytical skill. The virus discovery ended with a new principle from many small facts and principles. The Pythagorean Theorem started with an immutable triangle—the principle—and worked back to facts about the generalization. This is the way we think when we use mathematics in our everyday lives. We have a principle—our salary checks, for example—and we must derive facts about it—our budgetary items, for example. This is the analytical skill.

AN EXAMPLE FROM WRITING AND SPEAKING

The examples from the fields of writing and speaking are so numerous as to be obvious. For example, notes made in the form of speech outlines are to be found in Hyde Park, the home of the late President Franklin D. Roosevelt. He, as do most writers and speakers, first developed an outline of a speech or document (the generalization), and then filled out the outline with smaller bits and pieces (the specifics). This is clearly a case of deductive, or analytical, creative thinking.

The problem was: "How can I make a literary work or a speech from this outline?" The hypotheses were tested as added. When a word, phrase, clause, or sentence was selected as a tentative hypothesis, it was tested by saying it aloud or by thinking it through. Sometimes other persons help validate these hypotheses by listening. If the test of the hypothesis is positive, a conclusion is drawn, and the words, phrases, clauses, and sentences are used.

AN EXAMPLE FROM A MATHEMATICS CLASS

TEACHER: Prove that $\sqrt{3}$ is irrational.
STUDENT: We've never had that before.

STUDENT: What does "irrational" mean?

STUDENT: Doesn't it mean "not reasonable"?

TEACHER: Yes, that's right, but think in mathematical terms.

STUDENT: It says in the book that irrational means a non-repeating decimal. You can't express an irrational number as the quotient of two integers. But how do we prove that $\sqrt{3}$ is irrational?

TEACHER: You have to prove that if A^2 is divisible by 3, then A is divisible by 3.

STUDENT: I can't do that, either.

STUDENT: We can put any integer on the board like this:

$$A = \begin{cases} 3N \\ 3N+1 \\ 3N+2 \end{cases} \quad \text{then } A^2 = \begin{cases} 9N^2 \\ 9N^2 + 6N + 1 \\ 9N^2 + 12N + 4 \end{cases}$$

STUDENT: Only $9N^2$ is evenly divisible by 3, so A must be of the form 3N.

STUDENT: But this doesn't prove that $\sqrt{3}$ is irrational.

TEACHER: Think of a proof by contradiction.

STUDENT: All right. We'll assume that $\sqrt{3}$ is rational. Then $\sqrt{3}$ can be expressed in the form P/Q, and P and Q have no common factors. If $P/Q = \sqrt{3}$, then $P^2/Q^2 = 3$, and $P^2 = 3Q^2$.

STUDENT: Then P^2 is divisible by 3.

STUDENT: Our subproof is: "If A^2 is divisible by 3, then A is divisible by 3. Then P is divisible by 3."

STUDENT: We'll write $P = 3R$, where R is an integer. Now $P^2 = 9R^2$ and $P^2 = 3Q^2$. So $9R^2 = 3Q^2$.

STUDENT: Now $3R^2 = Q^2$. I multiplied by ⅓. So Q contains a factor of 3 because of our lemma. Now if P and Q both contain a factor of 3, they aren't reduced to the lowest of terms. This is a contradiction.

STUDENT: We wanted a contradiction. Our original assumption is false. Therefore, $\sqrt{3}$ is irrational.

In this example of deductive, or analytical, reasoning, the learners are going through the age-old mathematical activity of building a theorem out of a conjecture. That is, they are trying to add facts together to prove a generalization. The generalization had already been formulated, and they were attempting to justify it.

AN EXAMPLE FROM THE ENGLISH CLASS

TEACHER: What do you mean, The biggest difference between Frost and Sandburg is that they lived in different environments?

STUDENT: If Frost had lived in the Chicago area, he wouldn't have written about the woods on a snowy evening.

STUDENT: He would have if he were living two hundred years ago. But now there aren't any woods or animals around there.

STUDENT: What made the animals leave that part of the country?

TEACHER: What are the factors that limit your movements?

STUDENT: Money.

STUDENT: Deer don't use money. I think food and shelter would be important.

TEACHER: What sort of food and shelter do these animals need?

STUDENT: Hay or corn, I suppose.

STUDENT: We could look it up in the library.

STUDENT: Why not check with the Department of Conservation or the Department of Agriculture?

STUDENT: I'll volunteer to interview the local agent.

STUDENT: Some of us can write letters.

While this might be considered a far cry from a typical English lesson, the teacher recognized that the learners were interested enough to want to participate in some language-arts activities—interviewing and writing letters. The original problem can probably be explored after the students have accumulated the necessary information.

A CONCLUSION

Mathematics is a type of language. It is more properly grouped with the language arts than with the sciences. On the other hand, the natural and social sciences should be considered together. All science has social implications, and all social problems have scientific aspects.

The natural and the social sciences are both primarily synthetic studies, while mathematics and language arts are primarily analytical studies. Perhaps we need to take a hard look at our propensity to group mathematics and science together, and social science and English together. With this type of grouping, can we truthfully say that English does not become the tool of social studies? or that mathematics is not subsidiary to science?

Language and Critical Thinking

If we were to ask ourselves what tools we use in teaching, our immediate response would probably be to list things such as textbooks, television, charts, chalkboards, pencils and paper. A little more reflection would tell us that these items, although important, all depend upon another, more basic tool. This other tool is, of course, language. Language is the *primary* tool of instruction, the basic instrument used by teachers and learners in the vast majority of school tasks.

As teachers we spend a great deal of time and effort helping students to develop and refine their language skills. Classes in "English" or "Language Arts" or "Communication Skills" have the development of such skills as a major goal. Attention to these skills is also common in other classes. We have all heard the familar faculty-room dictum: "We are all teachers of English." The time and effort are well-spent, for students do become more proficient in their use of language as they progress in school.

Even though we may do a good job in teaching language skills, it may not be good enough. In spite of our efforts, we continue to find learners who, rather than mastering language, are mastered by it. Rather than using language as a tool for critical thinking, these students find language an obstacle to such thinking. Why does this happen? We might want to put *some* of the blame on the language tool itself: It isn't as precise as we might like. If our language were as precise as the "artificial" language of mathematics, many of the problems we encounter would disappear. But even though our language is not precise, it *is* our language and it *is* the basic instructional tool. Perhaps we need to recall the old adage that it is the poor carpenter who complains about his tools. The imprecision of the language is a fact: Our task is to help learners use the language tool well, and to do this they must be aware of its limitations. Language imprecision is generally a problem only when we use imprecise language as if it were precise.

THE MEANING OF WORDS

Sometimes the language we use in talking *about* language misleads us. What are we asking when we ask what a word means? This looks like a foolish question, for we all know that one of the things we are asking when we ask the meaning of a word is some notion of how that word is used intelligently. When we ask about meaning we are asking how informed people *use* the word. But sometimes we are not clear about this with students, and they then begin to assume that words have "real" meanings, or meanings which are quite independent of usage. There is, of course, no "real meaning" apart from usage, for a word can mean anything we agree to have it mean. To assume that words have meaning in and of themselves is to grant them a power which belongs to us. And it leads students to fruitless debates, such as the question of what "democracy" *really* means, or what "freedom" *really* means. These questions, which look like questions about words, hide the questions which may be more important—i.e., "What should a so-called democratic society be like?" or "How should we understand the concept of freedom?"

AMBIGUITY

When we say that a word is ambiguous, we mean that the same word has more than one meaning. In most cases this causes little difficulty. We can tell by the context in which the word appears which meaning is intended. If we ask, "Why didn't Johnny enter the race?", it is clear that, in most cases, we do not mean the human race. Similarly, if we say, "The pen is mightier than the sword," few would think we were speaking of pigpens or penitentiaries. This sort of ambiguity is a curiosity, but it is not really a problem.

Sometimes an ambiguity is not so clear, and this lack of clarity may get in the way of our thinking. Suppose a learner in your class said:

It is true that you do not like the principal. Teachers ought to tell their classes what is true. Therefore, you should tell our class that you do not like the principal.

Suppose further that the learner is correct. You detest your principal. Is the argument a strong one? If not, how should we explain to him *why* it is not? We would suspect at once that something is wrong with the argument—that such an argument cannot qualify as "critical thinking." Even if the "premises," or first two sentences, are true, the final sentence does not appear to be a justified conclusion. If we examine the argument carefully we notice that the meaning of the word "true" shifts from the first to the second sentence. In the first, "true" is apparently used so that the sentence carries the meaning, "It is a matter of fact that our teacher does not like the principal." "True" in the second sentence seems to mean, "Teachers ought to tell their classes things that are not false." This sentence does not suggest that teachers should tell *everything* which they know to be true, but only that they should not tell falsehoods.

The student's argument, as he has stated it, assumes that the term "true" means the same thing throughout the argument. In fact, he has changed the meaning in the middle of his argument. When this occurs in an argument—when a single word or phrase is used as if the meaning were constant when in fact the meaning shifts—the argument is faulty. There are many "shifty" words and phrases which we need to watch in our arguments. Some particularly tricky ones are relative terms such as "true," "good," "right," "duty," and "responsibility." Since most of us like labels, we can take the one generally used when talking about the sort of mistake made in the student's argument. The label is "the fallacy of equivocation."

We can help learners avoid equivocation by encouraging them to be especially careful with words whose meaning may vary with the contexts in which they are found. In the following example we can see a rather obvious equivocation on the word "right":

It is my right to refuse to join the PTA. I should, of course, do what is right. Therefore I should refuse to join the PTA.

The meaning of "right" in the first premise seems to be "privilege." In the second premise the meaning has shifted and appears to be "obligation" or "responsibility" or "duty" or "what is not wrong." If we were to pick the meaning in one premise and use it throughout the argument (and this is what is necessary if our argument is to be sound), the argument no longer seems plausible. For example, using the first meaning throughout, our argument would be:

It is my privilege to refuse to join the PTA. I should, of course, do what I am privileged to do. Therefore, I ought to refuse to join the PTA.

In the original argument we would probably accept the first two sentences as true. When we paraphrase, however, the second sentence becomes very odd. It just doesn't make sense to say that we should do what we are privileged to do because being privileged to do something normally means that we also have the privilege *not* to do it.

The argument fares no better if we take the meaning suggested in the second sentence. If the person has used "right" to mean "obligation" throughout the argument, the paraphrase would be:

It is my obligation to refuse to join the PTA. I should, of course, do what I am obliged to do. I should, therefore, refuse to join the PTA.

In this case we would be likely to doubt the truth of the first sentence. Although we might agree that a person has the *privilege* to refuse to join the PTA, few of us would argue that there is an *obligation* to refuse. Of course, the person who put forth the argument probably didn't intend that we take "right" to mean "obligation" in the first sentence. But neither did he intend that we take "right" in the second sentence to mean "privilege." The point is that he used the same term to mean one thing in the first sentence, and a very different thing in the second sentence.

What is the point of all this? Very simply, it is that, if we suspect equivocation, a useful way to go about checking is to paraphrase sentences in which the suspected term is used. If we find that the meaning of the term does seem to change within the argument, we should re-examine the argument using the intended meaning. The basic language fact is that a word may carry various meanings. Learners need to be aware of this imprecision in order to clarify their own thinking and to analyze the arguments of others. Whenever equivocation is suspected, it is important to determine whether the term means the same thing each time it appears in the argument. Imprecise language may encourage imprecise thought, but it need not.

Equivocation is not the only problem of the shifting meaning of words. Our language is such that it is possible to add, delete, or modify meaning simply by accenting words or phrases not intended to be accented, or by removing accents which are intended. The label we attach to such modification of meaning by altering the intended accent is "the fallacy of accent."

Examples of how meaning can be modified by accent are easy to find. Suppose your principal were to ask you to read to your class a new school rule. He hands you a sheet of paper on which the rule is written. You glance at the rule and find that it is a straightforward prohibition. The rule is:

No student shall throw stones through school windows.

We all understand what the rule means. But we should also understand that we can suggest new and additional meanings by adding accents.

Let us here indicate accent of a word with italics. Reading the rule aloud to your class, you place heavy accent on the word "student":

No *student* shall throw stones through school windows.

Is new meaning suggested? Are we now suggesting that stone-throwing is forbidden *only* to students? Is it all right for parents and teachers to throw stones through school windows? Certainly these meanings were not intended in the original rule, but they may indeed be *suggested* by altering or adding accent.

Other new meanings are suggested by accenting other words:

No student shall *throw* stones through school windows.

Are we now suggesting that it is permissible for students to drop, roll, or push stones through school windows?

No student shall throw *stones* through school windows.

Are we now not opposed to the throwing of teachers, parents, sticks or bottles through school windows?

No student shall throw stones *through* school windows.

Is it permissible for students to throw stones *around* the windows or bounce them off windows?

No student shall throw stones through *school* windows.

Does this now suggest permission to throw stones through the windows of churches or stores or homes?

No student shall throw stones through school *windows*.

Is the throwing of stones through doors and walls now permitted?

Of course there are legitimate uses of accent. That meaning may be modified by accent is a fact, not a problem. There is nothing wrong in using accent in writing or speaking to call attention to a point. It is when we are unaware that accent is modifying meaning that it becomes a problem. An example of this would be when we encounter italics which are added to a direct quotation. In such a case we need to remind ourselves that such accent may significantly modify the original meaning. Before we draw any conclusions which rest in part or whole on the quotation, we need to determine how, if at all, the original meaning has been modified by the new accent. And, of course, we should make it clear to learners that when they add italics to a direct quotation they should indicate that they have done this, for the meaning of the quotation is likely to change with the change in accent.

When we are dealing with the spoken rather than the written word, the effect of changing accent, and indeed even the fact that the accent has been changed, is much more difficult to determine. But even here we can help learners to improve their skill in recognizing where the accent falls in the spoken sentence and how this accent affects meaning. Once learners have developed such skills, they are better able to deal with the question of whether a particular accent placement is proper.

There is yet another kind of ambiguity in our language of which we should be aware. This has to do with the relationship between a whole and its parts, or between characteristics of individual members of a set or collectivity and the characteristics of the whole. The characteristics of individual parts are not necessarily characteristics of the whole, nor are the characteristics of the whole necessarily characteristics of individual parts.

Some examples might make this more clear.

Every student-council representative is a responsible person. The student council is therefore a responsible body.

Every member of the band is an excellent musician. Therefore this is an excellent band.

Each chapter of this history text is well-planned and organized. Therefore this history text is well-planned and organized.

In each of the above cases it seems clear that the conclusions do not follow. The quality in question may be the property of individual members and yet not be a property of the whole. The fact that the student council is composed of responsible students does not insure that this responsibility will transfer to the student council as a whole. The excellence of individual musicians does not guarantee that putting them together will result in an excellent band. And, of course, the planning and organization of individual chapters of a book do not provide us with sufficient evidence to make a judgment concerning the planning and organization of the book as a whole. Individual members or parts of a set or collectivity may have qualities which

are not necessarily qualities of the set or collectivity as
a whole. When we mistakenly assume that what is a
property of individual members or parts is necessarily
a property of a collectivity or set composed of those
parts, we label this mistake the "fallacy of composition."

Just as a collectivity may not, as a collectivity, share
the characteristics of individual members of that collectivity, so may the collectivity have characteristics
that are not shared by all its members. Notice the following:

Our student council is a responsible body. Therefore,
Johnny Jones, our representative, is a responsible person.

The Democratic (or Republican) Party is interested in
your welfare. Therefore, Mr. Smith, the Democratic (or
Republican) candidate is interested in your welfare.

This is a good class. Herbert Smith is in this class.
Therefore, Herbert Smith is a good student.

Each of these arguments is based on the notion
that the characteristics of a group or collectivity are
necessarily characteristics of individual parts or members. Our language seems to encourage this assumption. But our experience should tell us that language
misleads us in this regard. Take the first example
above. We know that a student council may, as a
whole, be a responsible body even though member
Jones is, by and large, an irresponsible student. And
in the second example we know full well that the commitment of a political party is no guarantee of the
commitment of an individual member of that party.
In the third example the case seems obvious: We do
talk about the general characteristics of classes with

no claim that these are the characteristics of every student.

The mistake of assuming that the characteristics of a collectivity are necessarily characteristics of each member or part is called the "fallacy of division." This mistake is very common, and is often used intentionally —e.g., by the politician who seeks to identify himself with the administration or some other group and then claim that he necessarily shares the attributes of that group. We must help learners become more aware of the problems involved in this whole-part reasoning.

EVALUATIVE WORDS

We use some words to describe things; others, to report our evaluations of things. If we say, "That tree is green," or, "That knife is sharp," or, "That student is asleep," we are simply describing things. We are not evaluating: We are not saying that we approve or disapprove of green trees, sharp knives, or sleeping students. But if you say, "That tree is green," and I say, "Good!" or "Groovy," you have described, and I have evaluated. My saying "Good!" or "Groovy!" is, in effect, to say, "I approve." And if you were to say, "That student is asleep," and I were to respond, "Terrible!" or "Shame!", or some such thing, I would again be evaluating what you described. In this case I would, in effect, be saying, "I disapprove." One author has called words we use to express approval "Yea words," and those we use to express disapproval, "Boo words."[1]

Now, if some words did nothing but describe, while

[1] Paul Nash, *Authority and Freedom* (New York: John Wiley and Sons, 1966).

others always meant "Yea!", and still others always meant "Boo!", we would have fewer problems with our language. The fact of the matter is, however, that many words which we commonly use *both describe and evaluate*. And these mixed words are the source of a great deal of difficulty. It is not that mixed words are bad, or that we should encourage learners to refrain from using them. It is important to recognize *when* they are being used and how their use may mislead us.

Suppose we hear the following in a classroom:

TEACHER: Albert, what are you doing with Cynthia's math paper?
ALBERT: Just looking at it.
BARBARA: He's not just looking at it. He's cheating!

What does the word "cheating" mean here? One thing which Barbara probably intends is to describe for the teacher what she thinks is happening. It may be that Barbara has observed Albert changing his answers so that they are the same as Cynthia's; or she may have noticed that Albert's paper was blank and that he is now rapidly copying the figures from Cynthia's paper. In short, "cheating" in this context does have some descriptive meaning. But is the term used *only* to describe? No. It also carries a "Boo!" meaning. When Barbara says that Albert is cheating, she is not only describing what is happening; she is saying that Albert ought *not* to do it; that she, Barbara, disapproves of what Albert is doing. If Barbara wished only to *describe* and not to evaluate, she might say, "Well, I see that Albert is transferring the figures from Cynthia's paper to his own." Did Barbara *intend* to evaluate as well as describe? This is the crucial question, and it is here that we see the problem of the mixed word. If Barbara intended to *both* describe and evaluate, there is no problem. But it is conceivable that she meant *only* to describe, and if this were her intent, then her choice of words is misleading. The point is, very simply, that we often tend to use mixed words as if they were purely descriptive, but the "Yea!" or the "Boo!" come through even though we do not intend them. Moreover, a word which is descriptive at one point in time may later take on "yea" or "boo" characteristics. Examples of this would be the terms "democracy" and "freedom," which are "yea" words as well as descriptive words in our culture. Some words which now say "Boo!", but which may have at one time been purely descriptive, are "Fascist," "Communist," and "slavery."

The mixed word often causes people to talk past one another. We have all heard debates over questions such as, "Is it ever right to murder?" or, "Should we ever approve of stealing?" In many cases the "boo" in the words "murder" and "steal" is often overlooked. One way of paraphrasing the questions would be to take out the mixed word—e.g., "Should we ever approve of the unlawful taking of another's property?" This is a much different question, for when the term "stealing" with its "boo!" is part of the question, a full paraphrase might be, "Should we ever approve of the unlawful taking of another's property? And, by the way, we do not approve of . . ."

This may seem to be much ado about very little. Still, it does appear that we should encourage learners to become aware of such linguistic pitfalls. If nothing else, such awareness should save them time that they might otherwise spend on fruitless debate. We our-

selves also need to guard against this problem, for
some of the very simple words we use in every class
may be mixed words.

Suppose we ask a question in a class. A learner answers the question and we respond, "Right!" We then
ask another question; another learner responds and
we say, "Wrong!" Think about the question some
more. What is it that we have said with our "Right!"
and "Wrong!"? If we are not careful we, and the
learners with us, will treat them as simply "Yeas" and
"Boos." But if we are really interested in helping
learners develop skills of critical thinking, we should
help them understand that the "rights" and "wrongs"
also give information. When the teacher says, "Right,"
the learner finds out not only that the teacher approves of his answer, but also that the answer is correct. And even if the teacher says, "Wrong," the
learner should come to regard the teacher's response
as an item of information. The learner has increased
his knowledge by finding out that his proposed answer
is incorrect. And this is a very useful bit of information for the learner as he continues to seek an answer
which is right.

SUMMARY

Our basic instructional tool is language. Although
we do a great deal to teach youngsters skills which will
allow them to use language more effectively, we still
find it commonplace that language, rather than aiding
the thinking process, hinders that process. Some
would argue that this is due to the imprecision of the
language. *That* the language is imprecise cannot be

doubted. But the imprecisions of our language, rather than being a ready excuse to explain away the problem, should themselves become an object of study. If we succeed in this, the language will remain imprecise, but the use of the language by the learners need not.

Uses of Language

We have seen that it is important for learners to recognize the imprecision in language in order that they may learn to use that language more effectively. However, becoming more sensitive to the imprecise nature of our language is not enough. Learners also need to become aware of the fact that many problems, although they involve language difficulty, are caused more by us than by our language. We use language for a number of different purposes, and too often we are clear neither about our purpose nor about how our usage of the language should be judged. Let us look at some of the major uses of language and how various uses can best be evaluated.

LANGUAGE USED TO INFORM

"That dog is mean."
"All students are lazy."
"Most teachers like children."
"Some crows are black."

The intent of each of the above statements is to provide us with some information. We will call this use of language—language used to inform, describe, or present arguments—the *informative* use. Clearly, such usage is a large part of the total language usage in the classroom, and sometimes we attempt to limit our usage to the informative. One example of such a limitation is furnished by the scientist. The scientist may attempt to avoid any use other than the informative in his scientific descriptions, explanations, and predictions. Statements such as "Copper conducts electricity," "Water freezes at 32° F.," and "The speed of light is greater than the speed of sound" are clearly informative statements: They make a claim or state information about the universe.

To say that a statement is informative should not be taken to mean that it is true. We may claim that we are informing, but our information may be false. But we can say of the informative use that an evaluation is one which seeks to determine *whether* the information is true or false. All informative statements are either true or false, even though we may not know which. To determine truth or falsity we look to those things about which the statement claims to inform us. Is the dog in question really mean? Is it a fact that all students are lazy? Is it true that most teachers like children? Are some crows black? Does copper conduct electricity? Examination of the dog, students, teachers, crows and copper will allow us, theoretically at least, to draw a conclusion about the truth or falsity of each of the statements. The fact that informative statements lend themselves to a true or false judgment helps us to identify usage as informative. The actual determination of truth or falsity provides the evaluation of the statement.

LANGUAGE USED TO DIRECT

"Go home!"
"Sit quietly."

"Obey the rules!"
"Come back here!"

When we hear imperatives such as these, we know that the speaker is not trying to inform us or to describe anything to us: He is trying to affect or direct our behavior. Several different terms have been used to describe this use of language. Let us here refer to it simply as the *directive* use. In the examples above, language is used to direct or *cause* some overt behavior. Directive use of language may serve also to *prevent* overt action:

"Don't walk on the grass!"
"Don't slam that door!"
"Don't talk without permission!"
"Don't run in the corridor!"

Whether language is used directively to cause or to prevent a certain kind of behavior, it is being used to influence behavior rather than to explain or describe.

When language is used to direct behavior rather than to explain or describe, does this mean we cannot evaluate the language usage? No, but it *does* cause the process of evaluation to differ from that applied in the case of the informative use. We cannot, for example, judge a directive as true or false. It would strike us as nonsensical if someone were to ask us to decide whether the utterance "Go home!" is true. But there are other judgments which can and should be made: The directive often calls for thinking quite as much as does the statement which claims to inform. The problem set by the directive is whether the action called for by the directive is reasonable or unreasonable, appropriate or inappropriate, justified or unjustified.

We can put this a slightly different way by saying that both the informative use of language and the directive use may create a situation calling for "problem-solving," or critical thinking. In the case of the informative use the problem is one of determining truth or falsity: With the directive use the problem is one of determining appropriateness or justification of the action which the directive encourages.

LANGUAGE USED TO EXPRESS EMOTION

A third major purpose for which language is used is to express feelings or attitudes or emotions, and in some cases to affect the feelings and attitudes of others. We will here refer to this as the *emotive* use. Perhaps the clearest case of the emotive use would be poetry, for much poetry has as its goal the communication of emotion. But the emotive use is found in many other contexts as well, and often plays a major role in such contexts as advertising, newspaper editorials, and political speeches.

Making judgments about the emotive use is a task that differs from both the "true-false" judgment of informative usage and the "appropriateness" judgment of directive usage. One evaluation which can be made of the emotive use is of the writer or speaker: Does he communicate the feeling or attitude which he attempts to communicate? We would here be asking whether the poet is an effective poet, the actor an effective actor, or the orator an effective orator. A second judgment of such usage has to do with whether the feeling or attitude is appropriate, both for the one who communicates and for those whom he seeks to influence. This evaluation differs from the judgment of the directive use in that the "appropriateness" refers to an emotion rather than an action. Thus, our concerns with the poet's emotive use of language are (a) whether he is successful in communicating the emotion, (b) whether the emotion he is expressing is appropriate, and (c) whether, when examined critically, we would share that emotion.

MIXED USAGE

Much of our language usage does not fall neatly into one or another of the three categories we have described above. Much of the time we put our language to work to do more than one thing at a time. We may wish at once to inform and affect action, or we may want to modify a person's emotions in order that a certain kind of behavior will follow. Many examples of such mixed usage can be found. A poem, for example, may give us information about the world (informative use), affect our feelings (emotive use), and cause us to behave in a certain way (directive use).

Another example of mixed usage which we encounter almost daily is the newspaper editorial. An editorial may be used to express attitudes or emotions held by the editor and to affect our own attitudes (e.g., I approve of political party X and detest political party Y). It may at the same time attempt to inform us about some matter (e.g., The candidate of party Y is incompetent). The editorial may also be intended to cause us to act in what the editor considers a desirable way (e.g., Don't vote for the party Y candidate). Such mixed usage may require more thinking and examination for an adequate evaluation. This does *not* mean that mixed usage is incorrect; indeed, it could be argued that the skillful mixture represents language usage at its best.

Deceptive mixed usage. Learners do need to be aware that mixed usage can be highly deceptive, and that it is not always an accident when a speaker or writer misleads us. The propagandist, in the modern sense of the term, may rely upon mixed usage to deceive intentionally. Or to put this another way, he may use language not to encourage thinking but to hide the fact that thinking is needed. He may, for example, encourage his readers or listeners to react to language used emotively as if it had been used to inform. Some political speeches furnish good examples of this. The old cliché that a certain politician has stated that he is *against* sin and *for* good government is a way of suggesting that language has been used to affect emotion with the hope that the emotional content will be treated as if it were informative. Thus, in the politician's speech there may be little or no informative content and no direct plea for action. Yet we may be influenced by the emotive content to behave *as if* we had been informed and *as if* this information justified or made appropriate a certain kind of behavior. In short, without really being given any good reasons for acting in a certain way, we may be swayed into such action by an emotional appeal. We are all in favor of what *we* consider to be "good government," and we are opposed to *our* notions of sin—and the politician, without communicating to us what *he* means by "good government" and "sin," hopes that his assertions will be emotively pleasing to us and that we will *assume* that his views and ours are the same.

We often deceive ourselves and others with mixed usage without intending to do so. We simply fall into deceptive mixed usage without recognizing it. Thus, we may quite innocently use an appeal to the emotions as if such an appeal served to inform.[1] Becoming more sensitive to language can help learners avoid mixed usage which is unintentionally deceiving. We certainly do not wish learners to deceive themselves and others unintentionally; indeed, it is to be hoped that we do not wish them to deceive at all.

PRACTICE IN ANALYZING MIXED USAGE

In many cases learners will face problems which involve analysis and evaluation of a mixed use of language. Such usage may be found in the poem in an English class, the editorial in a school newspaper, the classroom arguments for and against a proposed project, the class sociodrama, or the cartoon in the social studies text.[2] If learners are to respond intelligently

---

[1] This is an easy error to commit. We know that the fact that we are emotionally attached to an opinion or point of view does not provide any justification for that opinion: We can find all sorts of cases where people have been emotionally attached to erroneous beliefs. But we also know that emotional commitment can lead to action even when such commitment is not based on information. Perhaps this suggests that a continuing goal of the teacher ought to be to encourage learners to examine their emotional commitments to determine if they are based on adequate information.

[2] If such usage is *not* commonly found in some classrooms, it should be put in. Learners need to develop the skills necessary

to situations involving mixed usage, we should give
them practice in analyzing and judging such usage. It
is extremely important that they be able to distinguish
between the "emotive" content, the "informative" content, and the "directive" content, when such "contents" are mixed. In short, critical thinking about
language needs to precede other aspects of problem-
solving.

The Poem.   We have already said that poetry may
go beyond the expression or communication of emotion to inform and to recommend action. As an example, let us take the following stanzas from John Green-
leaf Whittier's "The Poor on Election Day":

> The proudest now is but my peer,
>   The highest not more high;
> Today, of all the weary year,
>   A king of men am I.
> Today, alike are great and small,
>   The nameless and the known;
> My palace is the people's hall,
>   The ballot box my throne!
> Who serves today upon the list
>   Beside the served shall stand;
> Alike the brown and wrinkled fist,
>   The gloved and dainty hand:
> The rich is level with the poor,
>   The weak is strong today;
> And sleekest broadcloth counts no more
>   Than homespun frock of gray.

Do these lines appeal to the emotions? Do they contain cognitive or informative content? Do they attempt

---

for the understanding and management of mixed usage, since
they will, in fact, encounter it outside, if not inside, the school.

to cause people to act in a certain way? Certainly we would want to answer "yes" to each of these questions. And if learners are studying such a poem they could be encouraged to examine the emotions, the information, and the actions suggested by the poem. Thus, a poem such as this could be used as an occasion to give learners practice in analyzing and evaluating mixed-language usage.

How might this be done? We might begin by having learners identify the contents of the poem—the emotive content, the informative content and the directive content. Once this is done, we could then ask the appropriate evaluation questions for each. The contents and the evaluation questions could be summarized as follows:

	CONTENT	EVALUATION QUESTIONS
Emotive	Whittier is expressing his emotional attachment to democracy. The poem also encourages the reader to share this attachment.	1. How effective is Whittier in communicating this emotion? 2. Is the emotion Whittier attempts to transmit appropriate and worthwhile?
Informative	Whittier is saying that all may vote in a democracy, that every man's vote is equal, etc.	Are these claims true?

	CONTENT	EVALUATION QUESTIONS
Directive	The directive content here is not as clear as are the emotive and the informative. Whittier does seem to suggest that citizens should participate in making decisions by exercising their right to vote.	Should every citizen exercise his right to vote?

We do not, of course, want to kill the enjoyment of a poem by overanalysis. We do, however, need to give learners the opportunity to recognize that poetry can be extremely powerful, not only as a means of expressing emotion but also as a way of informing and encouraging action. It is important that learners come to appreciate poetry, but appreciation must go beyond uncritical reading or uncritical assimilation of the author's feelings. It is likely that we would be willing to approve all of the contents in the Whittier lines quoted, but such a judgment properly *follows* rather than *precedes* analysis. If learners are encouraged to look only at the "feeling" content and accept or reject the entire content on this basis, they are not being encouraged to use critical thinking but are rather being subjected to emotional manipulation. There is, after all, no reason that a poem exalting totalitarian government cannot be quite as appealing to the emotions as is Whittier's poetic approval of democracy. But there is no need to be concerned about the poem which praises totalitarianism if we are able to extend the realm of critical thinking so that the learner responds intelligently to any poem.

Oratory. Oratory furnishes another excellent opportunity for learners to practice analyzing mixed usage. As an example, let us look at the oft-quoted closing lines of Patrick Henry's famous address to the Virginia Convention:

It is in vain, sir, to extenuate the matter. Gentlemen may cry, Peace, Peace—but there is no peace. The war is actually begun! The next gale that sweeps from the north will bring to our ears the clash of resounding arms! Our brethren are already in the field! Why stand we here idle? What is it that gentlemen wish? What would they have? Is life so dear, or peace so sweet, as to be purchased at the price of chains and slavery? Forbid it, Almighty God! I know not what course others may take; but as for me, give me liberty or give me death!

Certainly Patrick Henry had an unusual facility for using "mixed language" in a very effective way. When it is used so effectively we need to remind ourselves again that emotional fervor is not a substitute for information. Nor does strong emotional commitment provide sufficient reasons for action. Learners could be encouraged to analyze carefully such stirring speeches. With Henry's address they might be asked not only to separate the emotive from the informative and directive contents, but also to make a judgment as to whether the directive and emotive contents of the speech were appropriate at the time.[3]

[3] We would not say that Patrick Henry should have included more information. His purpose was to inspire and promote action, not to inform. But learners need to be aware that it would have been reasonable at the time to ask whether the situation did in fact justify Henry's feeling and make appropri-

The learners' summary of the content of the passage and some of the appropriate evaluation questions could take a form somewhat like the following:

	CONTENT	EVALUATION QUESTIONS
Emotive	Henry expresses strong feeling against reconciliation attempts; he is emotionally committed to liberty and is convinced that *both* liberty and peace are not possible.	1. How effective is Henry as an orator? Does he succeed in expressing his own emotional commitments and in encouraging others to share those commitments? 2. Are Henry's emotional commitments appropriate, given the context within which he spoke?
Informative	War has begun. Other colonists are already fighting. Henry seems to be asserting that the question is "either-or"—either become slaves or go to war.	Are Henry's assertions of fact true?

ate the action he recommended—just as it is reasonable today to ask whether any course of action recommended with great emotion is supported by fact as well as feeling.

Directive	The House of Burgesses should take a strong stand in preparing for war. Henry's purpose seems to be to convince others to accept his "liberty or death" position.	Was the course of action proposed by Patrick Henry the appropriate one?

Most learners will agree that the lines of Patrick Henry do affect their feelings. And most will probably agree that the situation did justify the action Henry recommended. But learners should come to see that this latter judgment should be made only *after* analysis and an examination of the facts, not *before*. If learners are encouraged to stop with the "feeling" content, they are in no position to make a judgment of the other contents: The emotional appeal of the weak cause can be as strong as that of the noble cause. What separates the two is not emotion but the supporting reasons and facts. Hitler's appeals to the German people to regain *lebensraum* were quite as effective as was Henry's plea for liberty. Our rejection of Hitler's position, or an acceptance of Patrick Henry's position, cannot be based on the question of whether holders of those positions are successful in affecting our emotions.

The list of examples of mixed-language usage could be greatly extended. The editorial in the local newspaper, the classroom discussion of a proposed project or field trip, the sociodrama, the school play, the television program on a social problem: In all of these

situations, and in many more, one is likely to find that
the first step in critical thinking is to be clear about
what is being said. Unless the tangle of language is
somehow straightened out, our problem-solving is
likely to go astray. And the needed careful and critical
use of language does not magically appear as the
learner develops: Rather, it needs to be taught, and is
perhaps taught best, through practice.

Pictures and Cartoons.   With poetry and oratory it
is relatively easy to determine how language is being
used. With pictures and cartoons we face a different
problem. The three kinds of contents are not made
explicit but are only suggested. This does not mean
that pictures and cartoons are beyond the realm of
critical thought. The opposite is probably true: When
a message (or messages) is only implicit, critical thinking is even more important.

Let us use as an example the political cartoon. With
the cartoon we have no, or few, words with which to
deal. What is the content of a cartoon? Well, the most
apparent and most explicit content is probably emotive. A cartoon may, for example, amuse or shock us
by lampooning political figures or ideas or organizations.

The cartoon also suggests informative content. For
example, a political cartoon may be intended to imply
that an absurdity pictured in a cartoon is but a slight
exaggeration of the policies of a certain politician, or
caricatures in the cartoon may be intended to be taken
as clarifications of real characteristics. Simplifications
or exaggerations may be used as if they throw light on
a subject rather than obscure it. Thus, informative content is suggested but not stated. To make a judgment

about this content, learners must first make the informative content explicit.

The primary purpose of many political cartoons is not simply to affect emotions or to inform. The major purpose is to affect or direct our actions. Thus, learners must go beyond evaluation of the emotive and informative content. They must question the action which the cartoon suggests as desirable.

We can see that it is important for learners to practice analyzing cartoons and other techniques which only suggest, rather than state, content. Communication devices such as cartoons and pictures, by themselves, can seldom be considered adequate information upon which to base action. The kinds of questions learners should ask about such techniques can be summarized as follows:

	CONTENT	EVALUATION QUESTIONS
Emotive	What feelings or emotions is the cartoonist attempting to communicate?	1. Does the cartoon effectively communicate the emotions? 2. Are the emotions appropriate?
Informative	What informative content seems to be suggested? Is there relevant information which is *not* suggested by the cartoon?	Is the suggested informative content true or false?

	CONTENT	EVALUATION QUESTIONS
Directive	Does the cartoon seem to suggest that some action should be taken? If so, what action?	Is the action which the cartoon encourages warranted?

The purpose of raising such questions is to enable and encourage learners to go beyond the "feeling" content when they encounter communication techniques which are used to inform and direct. It is not that something is *wrong* with the use of techniques such as the cartoon: It is rather that learners need to develop the skills of responding to such techniques intelligently. Failure to develop such skills makes one easy prey for the cartoonist or propagandist.

SUMMARY

Language is a necessary tool in the critical-thinking process, and this tool can be improved by conscious practice. We have noted three major categories of language use: the informative, the emotive, and the directive. There is an appropriate method of evaluation for each of the three categories. To evaluate informative usage, our task is to find whether the informative content is true or false. With the directive use, we look not to the language but to the action recommended and seek to determine whether such action is warranted. In the case of the emotive use, we can ask if the emotion has been effectively communicated and if the emotion itself is appropriate.

Often we find that in actual use these categories are mixed, that language is often used to serve more than one purpose at the same time. Such mixed usage is perfectly proper. It makes evaluation more complex, and makes it more important that learners acquire skills in analyzing such usage.

We encounter further problems with techniques of communication which suggest meaning which goes beyond the language actually used. Examples of such techniques might be pictures and cartoons. With such techniques it is very important that learners develop skills of analysis and evaluation. Thoughtful evaluation of the cartoon, for example, requires that the learner examine the *suggested* content as well as the *explicit* content.

Logic and Critical Thinking

We have been discussing the importance of helping learners develop skills in using language and in evaluating the language usage of others. This is important, for our "language tool" may either aid or obstruct the thinking process. But language skills are not enough. We have all encountered persons who are skillful in using language but who draw unwarranted conclusions or are convinced by weak arguments or make mistakes in the reasoning process itself. Such persons apparently have not developed the skill of determining whether an argument follows the rules of logic. The ability to apply basic rules of logic is a necessary skill which must be developed by learners if they are to avoid making mistakes in the reasoning process.

WHAT IS A "LOGICAL" ARGUMENT?

When we say that an argument is a *good* argument we may be saying that it meets two criteria. One criterion may be that the conclusion of the argument should be warranted or true. The second criterion is that the argument should follow a correct logical form. We might state this second criterion in a slightly different way: A good argument follows the rules of the game of logic. This is what we mean by a logical argument: An argument is logical if the rules of logic have not been violated. Thus, logic provides us with *some* of the rules of the game of critical thinking: the rules of argument form.

We can evaluate the form of an argument without in any way considering the content. An argument which follows correct logical form is called a *valid* argument; an argument which violates that form is referred to as *invalid*. To evaluate the *content* of an argument we must determine whether the statements in the argument are true, and this task is not to be accomplished by simply referring to the rules of logic. The two evaluations—one of form (validity) and the other of content (truth)—come together in this way: If an argument is valid *and* if the premises are true, then the conclusion must be true. Generally we are concerned with both of these judgments. In this chapter, however, our concern is primarily with judgments of logical form, with the validity of arguments rather than their truth.

In our everyday discussions, in classrooms and out, we often encounter arguments which do not follow correct logical form. The logical errors are commonly called *fallacies*. We could not possibly list all the kinds of fallacies which can be made, for there is simply no limit to the number of ways we can arrive at invalid conclusions. There are, however, some *common* mistakes, or fallacies, we can recognize and guard against. We have already examined some "fallacies of ambiguity" which arise because of the imprecision of our language. We now turn to fallacies which result from mistakes in reasoning. The skill of recognizing fallacious arguments should help both the teacher and the learner in the critical-thinking process.

FALLACIES OF RELEVANCE

Fallacies which occur in our everyday use of language are called *informal fallacies*. We have already discussed some informal fallacies termed "fallacies of ambiguity," which arise from the imprecise nature of language. We now turn to informal fallacies which are due to inconsistencies in thought: These are called "fallacies of relevance." In arguments containing fallacies of relevance the premises, or reasons given to support the conclusion, do not provide *logical* support. The premises are not logically relevant to the conclusion. In other words, the conclusion does not logically follow from the premises. In a fallacious argument it is possible that the premises or reasons may be true and yet the conclusion may be false, since there is no *logical* connection between the premises and the conclusion.

One of the problems with fallacious arguments is that they do often convince people. An invalid argument may be extremely persuasive if we do not have the skill to analyze it. Arguments often convince not because they are *logically* sound but because they are psychologically or emotionally appealing. Psychological or emotional reasons for accepting a conclusion *may* be justifiable reasons, but this does *not* make such reasons logical. We should not confuse an argument which is psychologically appealing with one which is logically sound. The fallacies of relevance are cases in which such a confusion is found. Let us look at some examples.

Appeal to force. Does might make right? This is

an ancient question, and the answers which have been given historically do not all agree. When we ask this question with reference to logical argument, however, the answer is a firm "no": Might or force is not a substitute for logical argument. Yet we do need to notice that force is sometimes allowed to masquerade as logical argument. Notice the following "arguments":

You ought to do as I say in this class [proposed conclusion]. Do I need to remind you that you can be sent to the principal for disciplinary action? [reason or premise].

Senator, you ought to support our position on the matter [proposed conclusion]. As voters we will remember your stand when we go to the polls [reason or premise].

Several teachers have questioned whether they should be present at the PTA meeting [proposed conclusion]. Perhaps they need to be reminded that our PTA can greatly influence a teacher's success in this community [reason or premise].

None of these examples represents a sound *logical* argument: Indeed, the reason given for each conclusion is logically irrelevant to that conclusion. Yet it is clear that the reasons may be psychologically or emotionally relevant. When we find threat or force suggested as reasons for accepting a conclusion, we should recognize that what we have is *not* a logical argument but rather a rejection of such an argument. The appeal to force is often used when rational argument has failed to convince or when no logical argument can be found to support the conclusion.

To say that an appeal to force is not a proper part of logical argument does not mean that such an appeal is always wrong. It may be perfectly proper for a parent to threaten the small child with a spanking for crossing the street, or for a teacher to threaten the recalcitrant learner with a trip to the principal's office. It is simply that the appeal to force does not warrant the acceptance of the proposed conclusion as a *logical* conclusion. If learners are to be successful in thinking through arguments, they need the skill to distinguish between arguments which are *logically* sound and those that convince by emotional or psychological appeal.

Argument directed to the man.   It is very common in argument, particularly in heated argument, for the participants to stray from the issue and attack one another verbally. Arguments such as the following are often heard:

Mr. Black has suggested that no salary increases should be given to teachers this year because of our local financial crisis. This suggestion should not be taken seriously, because Black has a long record of attempting to block progress in this community. His position on teachers' salaries reflects his narrow outlook and limited understanding. Those who are aware of his public record and his motives will reject his suggestion because of its source.

Joe Jones's father called me to complain that I was giving Joe too much homework. He certainly shouldn't be criticizing teachers, since he didn't even graduate from high school and probably can't read a newspaper. He's probably just complaining because he's too lazy to make Joe work. If he would learn to mind his own business, it would help a great deal.

What is the purpose of such arguments? They seem to

attempt to discredit the source or holder of an idea or proposition rather than the idea or proposition itself. The assumption seems to be that if the holder of an idea can be discredited, the idea itself can be rejected. This is another example of psychological or emotional appeal rather than logical appeal. We can see this through a careful examination of the examples.

In the first example the question is whether teachers should or should not be given salary increases. Black's motives and public record are not relevant to this question. In the second example the question is whether or not Joe Jones is being expected to do too much homework. The educational level of Joe's father and the extent of his literacy are beside the point. Such arguments are fallacious because discrediting the source does not answer the question: Rather, the question is simply ignored. It may well be that the teachers in the first example should be given salary increases. And it may be that Joe Jones's father is wrong about the homework. But if one wants to show that the arguments of Mr. Black and Mr. Jones are in error, he must direct *his* arguments to *their* arguments, not to the character of the men themselves.

We all know, of course, that arguments-directed-to-men are widely used and are quite effective. If they were not effective perhaps they would be used less by advertisers, politicians and propagandists. Learners need to develop the skill to analyze such arguments, and to recognize that this fallacious argument form is often used to cover an otherwise weak argument. With such skill they will neither accept nor reject an argument because of its source.

Argument from ignorance. We sometimes encounter arguments which cannot, at the present time at least, be proved either true or false. With such arguments we frequently find the claim that if a conclusion cannot be shown to be true it must therefore be false, or that if a conclusion cannot be shown to be false it must therefore be true. But lack of refutation is not proof, nor is lack of proof refutation. To assume that an argument which cannot be proved wrong is therefore right, or that an argument which cannot be proved right is therefore wrong, is to base a conclusion on ignorance: ignorance of how the argument can be proved or refuted. Some examples of this fallacy follow.

This book should not be allowed in our high-school library, because it encourages immoral behavior. Despite what my critics say, they have been unable to disprove this fact. Thus, it is clear that this book and others like it do have such an effect upon our students and therefore ought to be taken from the library shelves.

Proponents of federal aid to education continue to argue that such aid will not lead to federal control. Where is their proof? They have none, and thus we must conclude that their argument fails. Federal aid leads inevitably to federal control.

In the first example the inability to disprove is taken as proof; in the second, lack of proof is taken as refutation. Both are examples of the fallacy of the argument from ignorance. What *should* we conclude from our inability to prove or refute? One conclusion we might draw is that the argument is "open." By an open argument here, we mean one which we cannot, at present at least, logically prove or disprove.

If this fallacy is discussed in a classroom, it is likely

that some perceptive learners will raise some objections and give as evidence what seem to be exceptions to this fallacy. One such seeming exception is our "innocent until proven guilty" notion of justice. But when we say a person is innocent until proven guilty we do not intend this as a logical statement nor as a statement of fact. Rather, we mean that the ethical thing to do is to treat all persons *as if* they are innocent until they are proved guilty. As a matter of logic, innocence or guilt is quite independent of proof. As a matter of law, guilt is asserted only when proved "beyond reasonable doubt." And where this is not proved in our courts, we would be more precise by saying that the person *had not been found guilty* rather than saying that he had been found *not guilty*. But our point here is simply that we often accept a lack of proof as refutation, but when we do this our reasons are moral or ethical, not logical. These "exceptions" are important, for they reflect some of our cherished values. Learners should be encouraged to find such value positions and to distinguish between such value positions and statements of fact.

Appeal to pity.   It is common to find arguments which encourage us to accept conclusions on the basis of pity rather than on logical grounds. The appeal to pity is used frequently as a "last resort" argument when the logical argument is weak or is failing to convince. Most teachers are familiar with appeals to pity such as the following:

I know I didn't do well on this test. I tried to study last night but my parents and brothers and sisters kept interrupting me. I would have studied earlier but my eyes have been bothering me. I have been trying hard to learn but my paper route takes so much time, etc., etc. I hope you will remember these things when you grade my paper.

I think Suzy should be elected to the Student Council. She has already had so many disappointments this year. She would have been chosen as a class officer had she not been ill, and she would be more active in other school activities if she did not have to work so hard at home, etc., etc.

In both of the above examples we are encouraged to accept a conclusion on the basis of pity rather than logical argument. While it may be extremely difficult to protect ourselves from such an appeal (if we really wish to be so protected), it is an easy fallacy to recognize. The clear appeal to the emotions may be psychologically compelling, but it requires little examination to show that such an argument is not convincing from the standpoint of logic. What may be more difficult is the decision of whether we wish to be guided by emotions or by logic and reason. In any case, learners should be encouraged to practice using reason in determining when and under what conditions the appeal to pity is appropriate.

Fallacy of false cause. When we observe in our experience that one event follows another, we often assume that the first event *caused* the second. Of course, in many cases there is no such connection between the two events: It is a matter of coincidence that the two occurred in a particular order. When we assume a causal connection where none exists we are committing the fallacy of false cause. This fallacy is the source of much superstition, in our own society as well as in those societies we tend to regard as primitive. In order to avoid this fallacy we should hesitate to claim a causal connection between events until an attempt has been made to disprove such a connection. We might suspect the fallacy of false cause in each of the following examples.

It's better not to sleep the night before exams. I know several people who did not sleep before this exam, and they all passed.

I have proof that a rabbit's foot will bring good luck. I began carrying a rabbit's foot last week, and this morning I found a five-dollar bill.

A study of Latin makes the study of English much easier. I studied Latin in high school and have not had as much trouble with college English as I expected.

In each of the above cases we have the assumption that there is a causal connection between the earlier and the later event. Now, if it can be shown that the second event does not necessarily follow the first—that the first may occur without being followed by the second—the causal connection has been disproved. For example, we might be able to find a student who did not sleep and failed the exam; a person who studied Latin in high school and had more difficulty in college English than expected. Such cases would be evidence that there is no causal connection. Our point here is that whenever a causal connection is suggested, we should look for further evidence to either support or reject the belief that there is such a connection. To fail to look for further evidence may lead us to accept arguments which are analogous to: "Night follows day; therefore, day *causes* night."

LOGIC AND CRITICAL THINKING

The complex question. We are sometimes asked questions which we cannot answer in the form in which they are asked without committing ourselves on an unasked question. Or to put this in a slightly different way, the complex question is one which is asked as if it were a simple question, when, in fact, it implies that a previous question has been asked and answered. Each of the following is a complex question.

(a) Why do teachers give assignments which are too long?

(b) How long will we continue to throw money away on foreign aid?

(c) Why have students lost their sense of responsibility?

(d) When will parents cease criticizing the schools unfairly?

All of these follow the pattern of the classic question: "Have you stopped beating your wife?" The very form in which this question is asked suggests that an affirmative answer has already been given to the question: "Have you been guilty of wife-beating?" Unless the person to whom the complex question is asked agrees to the affirmative answer to the prior question, he cannot answer the complex question "yes" or "no." In common parlance, he is "damned if he does and damned if he doesn't." But this does not mean that the complex question is difficult to guard against. Learners need to develop the ability to recognize complex questions and isolate the prior questions. In the

above examples the prior questions are quite easy to
identify:

(a) *Complex question:* Why do teachers give assignments which are too long?

    Prior question: Do teachers give assignments
which are too long?

(b) *Complex question:* How long will we continue to
throw money away on foreign
aid?

    Prior question: Are we throwing money away
on foreign aid?

(c) *Complex question:* Why have students lost their
sense of responsibility?

    Prior question: *Have* students lost their sense
of responsibility?

(d) *Complex question:* When will parents cease criticizing the schools unfairly?

    Prior question: Are parents guilty of unfairly
criticizing the schools?

Once the complex question is recognized as such and
the prior question is identified, the problem disap-
pears. We can then begin *with the prior question* as
we would with any other question.

Appeal to the gallery. It is quite common in our
society today to find many attempts to persuade us to
accept a conclusion on the grounds that most of our
fellow citizens accept it. Such attempts are often called

the "appeal to the gallery" or the "appeal to the people." There are many variations of this appeal. One of these is the appeal to "common sense." We have all heard arguments like the following:

It is only common sense that students will not accept responsibility. We all know that they will take advantage of any situation in which they are not closely supervised. Therefore, students should always be closely supervised.

Everybody knows that children are not learning the fundamentals as well as they did a generation ago. Common sense alone will tell us that there are too many frills in the schools and that a return to the 3 Rs is needed.

These are examples of the appeal to common sense. Such arguments often begin with, "It is only common sense that . . ." or, "We all know that . . ." The goal of this appeal seems to be to persuade that (1) the majority already accepts the proposed conclusion, and (2) the fact that the majority holds this conclusion is sufficient reason for its acceptance. Whether the majority does, in fact, accept the conclusion really makes no difference. Even if a conclusion is accepted by the vast majority, this is not in itself reason to be persuaded: The majority *can* be wrong. A show of hands may give us an indication of how opinions are shared, but it is not a substitute for critical thinking or logical argument.

A second form of the appeal to the gallery is the well-known and much used "bandwagon" technique. Some examples of this technique are:

Buy brand X. Everyone is using it.

The whole gang is voting for Johnny. Why don't you?

You're the only one in the class who doesn't enjoy poetry. Since everyone else volunteers to recite a few lines, don't you think you should too?

In each of these examples we find the basic form, "Everyone is doing it, so why don't you?" As arguments, these are of course fallacious, for they attempt to persuade by appealing to the claim that the conclusion is accepted by a majority of others. Of course, we are all very familiar with this technique, and we have little difficulty in recognizing its use. Yet we must also admit that it is enormously successful, and hence learners may need practice in identifying and examining the bandwagon technique in use. We are perhaps most accustomed to finding this technique used by advertisers and politicians, but we must admit that it is no stranger to classrooms.

The glittering generality. The "glittering generality," sometimes called the "rosy-glow device," is a technique in which the speaker or writer proceeds as if he were informing when, in fact, he is using terms to appeal to the emotions. We are all familiar with examples such as the following:

Vote for Candidate Smith. He loves his country. He stands for good government, honest administration and responsible economic policy.

This course should be required of all students. It encourages moral behavior, good citizenship and warm human relationships.

To what extent do these examples inform? How

are we to understand "good government," "responsible economic policy," "moral behavior," or "good citizenship"? Few of us would be opposed to any of these things so long as we were the ones deciding what the general phrases meant. And deciding what the phrases mean is the issue. That Candidate Smith favors good government is a reason to support him only if we agree with Smith as to what good government is. And we are all in favor of good citizenship, but this is only important if we agree about what good citizenship is. The point is that we are often misled by the "glittering generality." Most of us have an emotional commitment to the meaning *we* assign to a generality such as "good government" or "good citizenship." The "glittering generality" technique encourages us to *assume* uncritically that our meaning is shared by those seeking our support. Whether this is true can be decided only by making the meaning explicit. In short, we need to help learners become aware of those terms which cause a "rosy glow" within them. Such a glow ought to be taken as a warning that critical thinking is needed.

Appeal to authority. It is sometimes argued that a conclusion should be accepted because it is supported by persons considered to be authorities on the question at issue. There are many situations in which we would consider such an appeal reasonable. For example, we are likely to accept medical conclusions agreed upon by physicians or conclusions about our automobile engines agreed upon by competent mechanics. We increasingly need and value the opinions of experts, and in many cases we accept these opinions as sufficient evidence to support conclusions. Sometimes, however, we appeal to a person who is an expert in one field about some matter in a different field. This sort of appeal is a mistake. We need to keep in mind, and encourage learners to keep in mind, that there is no such thing as an "expert in general." The expertise of a baseball player does not imply expertise in evaluating razor blades; the outstanding theorist in nuclear physics is not necessarily an expert on the politics of disarmament; the submarine expert is not automatically an expert on questions of public education. Thus, learners need to become aware that any appeal to authority should be prefaced by an examination to determine whether the suggested authority is, in fact, an authority *on the question at hand.*

It is not always clear whether a person's expertise qualifies him to give an expert judgment on a question. There are many contemporary problems which are so wide in scope that no one specialization is adequate for expert judgment on the whole problem. For example, who are the experts on Medicare? On federal aid to education? On the problems of ghetto schools? Each of these problems goes beyond the narrow expertise of the "professionals." The Medicare issue is *in part* a medical question (hence, members of the medical profession are experts), but it is also in part an economic question and a moral, or ethical, question. Similarly, federal aid to education is in part an educational question, in part an economic and political question. The experts themselves may not clearly distinguish between when they are speaking as experts and when they are speaking only as concerned citizens. To evaluate the information offered by these experts, we must make a judgment about the limits of their expertise. Physicians may be qualified experts on medical questions, but this does not mean that they are experts on questions of broad social or economic policy. Educators may be experts on educational questions, but this expertise does not necessarily extend to questions of economics and politics.

There is yet another difficulty with the appeal to authority. Even when persons are accepted as authorities, their opinions may conflict with one another. When this occurs we see again that there is no substitute for critical thinking, and even the appeal to experts cannot be an abdication of our responsibility to attack our problems intelligently.

Logical fallacies and the teacher. If we are to encourage learners to develop skills in critical thinking, part of our task is to aid them in identifying and avoiding mistakes in reasoning. The kinds of mistaken arguments which we have been discussing are not restricted to life outside the school: They can be found in classrooms at all levels of schooling and in all subject-matter areas. As pointed out in earlier chapters, critical thinking does not develop automatically, but can be and should be taught. Logical reasoning is a part of critical thinking. Too often we assume that logical reasoning just develops, that learners pick up logic by some form of intellectual osmosis. It may be true that *some* logic "is just picked up" or "rubs off," but certainly this process could be improved by some purposeful teaching. This does not mean that we need more courses in logic, but that logic could and should be taught as a part of other subject matter and recognized as a crucial part of the critical-thinking process.

LOGICAL FORM

A valid logical form. We said earlier that logic is the study of argument *form,* not argument *content.*

We will now look at some deductive-argument forms which can be used to evaluate arguments. An argument form is valid if, and only if, it is impossible for the premises to be true and the conclusion false. Let us illustrate this with what is called a "hypothetical syllogism."

Major premise:　If John has taught all day, then he is too tired to attend the PTA meeting.

Minor premise:　John has taught all day.

Conclusion:　Therefore, John is too tired to attend the PTA meeting.

The form this argument takes is a valid one. Any argument which follows this form is valid. Thus, in any argument which takes this form it is impossible for the conclusion to be false *if* the premises are true. Of course the premises may be false, but that is not our concern here.

But what is the *form* of the above argument? We can see the form more clearly if we replace the content with arbitrary symbols. The symbols we will use here are the letters "p" and "q," which are conventional logical symbols. Let "p" replace "John has taught all day," and "q" replace "John is too tired to attend the PTA meeting." Using these symbols as replacements throughout, our argument is as follows:

Major premise:　If (John has taught all day) **"p"**, then (he is too tired to attend the PTA meeting) **"q"**.

Minor premise:　(John has taught all day.) **"p"**

Conclusion: (John is too tired to attend the PTA meeting.) "**q**"

The words of the above argument can now be removed in favor of our symbols. We now have the following:

Major premise: If "**p**," then "**q**"

Minor premise: "**p**"

Conclusion: Therefore "**q**"

We now see the argument form. This is a standard valid argument form. This particular form is referred to in logic as *modus ponens*. Now, *any argument of this form is a valid argument.* Hence, any "substitution instance"—*any* argument content put into this form—is a valid argument. Some examples of "substitution instances"—hence, valid arguments—follow:

A. *Major premise:* (If teachers explain assignments adequately) = If **p,** "**p**", the (students will do then their homework). "**q**" **q**

Minor premise: (Teachers explain assignments adequately.) "**p**" = **p**

Conclusion: Therefore, (students will do their homework.) "**q**" = **q**

B. *Major premise:* (If Johnny can't read) = If **p,** "**p**", then (the schools then have failed). "**q**" **q**

Minor premise: (Johnny can't read.) "**p**" = **p**

| *Conclusion:* | Therefore, (the schools have failed). "q" | = | q |

C. *Major premise:*   If (we are interested in true education) "p", then (we must place more emphasis on the 3 Rs). "q"   = If p, then q

Minor premise: (We are interested in true education.) "p"   =   p

Conclusion: (We must place more emphasis on the 3 Rs.) "q"   =   q

D. *Major premise:*   If (teachers' salaries are adequate) "p", then (instruction will improve). "q"   = If p, then q

Minor premise: (Teachers' salaries are adequate.) "p"   =   p

Conclusion: Therefore, (instruction will improve). "q"   =   q

In each of the examples we have a valid argument simply because the argument follows a valid form. Thus, in making a judgment about an argument it is important to examine the form the argument takes. By examining the form we can determine whether the argument is valid.

When we seek to discover whether a conclusion is *true* we must go beyond the form of the argument. A valid argument guarantees a true conclusion only if the premises are true. But whether the premises are true cannot be determined by an examination of the argument alone. Let us look again at our first example. To determine whether the premises are true we would need to find out:

(1)   Whether teaching all day does, *in fact,* fatigue John to the extent that he is then too tired to attend PTA meetings.

(2)   Whether it is true that John has taught all day.

If we find that the premises are true, then, and only then, can we say we have *both* a valid argument and a true conclusion. Thus, we test for validity by examining the form of the argument. To test for truth we must go beyond an examination of the argument itself.

A fallacious logical form.   Just as there are valid forms of reasoning, so are there some invalid forms. Not *every* invalid form presents a problem, for some are obviously fallacious. The ones that do present problems are those that bear a superficial resemblance to valid forms. One such invalid form, generally labeled the "fallacy of asserting the consequent," resembles *modus ponens.* The form this fallacy takes as compared to *modus ponens* is:

	Modus Ponens	*Fallacy of Asserting the Consequent*
Major premise:	If "p", then "q"	If "p", then "q"
Minor premise:	"p"	"q"
Conclusion:	"q"	"p"

Why is asserting the consequent invalid? Simply because the truth of the premises does not guarantee the truth of the conclusion. Perhaps this can be seen more clearly if we put the content back into the form. Let us rewrite some of our examples to fit this invalid form.

A. *Major premise:* If (we are interested in true education) **"p"**, then (we must place more emphasis on the 3 Rs). **"q"**

Minor premise: (We must place more emphasis on the 3 Rs.) **"q"**

Conclusion: (We are interested in true education.) **"p"**

B. *Major premise:* If (teachers' salaries are adequate) **"p"**, then (instruction improves). **"q"**

Minor premise: (Instruction does improve.) **"q"**

Conclusion: (Teachers' salaries are adequate.) **"p"**

C. *Major premise:* If (Johnny can't read) **"p"**, then (the schools have failed). **"q"**

Minor premise: (The schools have failed.) **"q"**

Conclusion: (Johnny can't read.) **"p"**

These examples are now all substitution instances of the invalid form

If **"p"**, then **"q"**
"q"
Therefore **"p"**

If we examine each of these examples, we can see that it is logically possible for the premises to be true and the conclusion false. Let us take the example of teachers' salaries. Suppose we are agreed that the first premise is true: If teachers' salaries are adequate, instruction improves. Let us further suppose that it is true that instruction is improving. What can we conclude? Certainly we *cannot* conclude that salaries are adequate, for adequate salaries may be only one of many things which would lead to improved instruction. Better supervision, better working conditions, more adequate materials, and many other factors might well lead to better instruction. To put this in slightly different words, the first premise claims that adequate salaries are *sufficient* to bring about improved instruction—i.e., with adequate salaries instruction will improve. It does not say that adequate salaries are *necessary* for improved instruction—i.e., instruction may be improved without adequate salaries. The point is that in each of the examples there may be causes other than the specific antecedent (the "p" statement) which could account for the occurrence of the consequent (the "q" statement). Hence, the conclusions in these three examples are not logical conclusions.

And another valid logical form. Another common *valid* logical form is:

Major premise:	If "p", then "q"
Minor premise:	not "q"
Conclusion:	not "p"

This valid form is referred to as *modus tollens*. Again, since this is a valid form, any substitution instance will also be valid. Some examples of substitution instances are:

A. *Major premise:* If (the schools are controlled by federal authorities) **"p"**, then (schools fail to meet local needs). **"q"**

Minor premise: (It is not true that schools fail to meet local needs.) **"not q"**

Conclusion: (It is not true that the schools are controlled by federal authorities.) **"not p"**

B. *Major premise:* If (history is properly taught) **"p"**, then (students will appreciate the national heritage). **"q"**

Minor premise: (It is not true that students appreciate the national heritage.) **"not q"**

Conclusion: (It is not true that history is properly taught.) **"not p"**

In either of these examples we would find it logically impossible to hold that the premises were true but the conclusion false. Any argument at all which is a substitution instance of this form is valid. If the premises of such an argument are true, the conclusion must be true.

And another fallacious form. An invalid argument form which superficially resembles the *modus tollens* form is:

Major premise: If **"p"**, then **"q"**
Minor premise: not **"p"**
Conclusion: not **"q"**

This form is commonly referred to as the *fallacy of denying the antecedent*. Rewriting the preceding examples to fit this form would give us the following invalid arguments:

A. *Major premise:* If (the schools are controlled by the federal authorities) **"p"**, then (schools will fail to meet local needs). **"q"**

Minor premise: (It is not true that the schools are controlled by federal authorities.) **"not p"**

Conclusion: (It it not true that schools will fail to meet local needs.) **"not q"**

B. *Major premise:* If (history is properly taught) **"p"**, then (students will appreciate the national heritage). **"q"**

Minor premise: (It is not true that history is properly taught.) **"not p"**

Conclusion: (It is not true that students appreciate the national heritage.) **"not q"**

These arguments are fallacious because it would be possible for the premises to be true and the conclusions false. In the first example the conclusion may be false simply because there are many factors which could cause schools to fail to meet local needs. Hence, even if we agree that the premises are true, we must admit that there remains a possibility that the conclusion is false. The same is true in the second example: Factors other than the proper teaching of history could lead students to appreciate the national heritage. The argument is invalid because the truth of the premises does not guarantee the truth of the conclusion.

LOGICAL FORM IN LENGTHY ARGUMENTS

The basic rules of logic apply no matter how lengthy or involved an argument may be. Thus far we have used short and relatively uninvolved arguments for the sake of simplicity. However, an entire book, article, speech, etc., may be constructed on a framework of either a valid or invalid logical form. For example, a newspaper editor may write a column in which he assumes that:

If taxes are too high, then corporate profits will decline.

and goes on to assert that

Profits are declining.

and then concludes:

Taxes are too high.

What is the form of argument in this editorial? It is:

Major premise: If "p", then "q"
Minor premise: "q"
Conclusion: "p"

And this form is, of course, the fallacy of asserting the consequent. The point is that we need to remember, and to help learners understand, that the rules of logic apply whether we are dealing with a three-line argument or a three-volume set.

MAKING GENERALIZATIONS

We noted earlier that the truth of the premises of an argument is not determined by appealing to the rules of logic. Very often a premise of an argument is a generalization, a claim about all members of a class or a set. When can we be certain that such a generalization is true? Only when we have examined all the members of the class or set about which we are generalizing. In many situations, however, we find that we must make a tentative generalization even though we cannot possibly examine all members of the set. In such situations the soundness of our generalizations depends upon the strength of our evidence—i.e., we cannot know whether our generalization is true, but we can make a judgment concerning the strength of our evidence.

The process of examining evidence for the generalizations we make is a crucial part of critical thinking. A common and serious reasoning error, in classrooms and out, is making generalizations based on evidence which is clearly insufficient without recognizing the inadequacy of that evidence. The old quip, "All Indians walk in single file—at least the one I saw did." may strike us as humorous, but we need to recognize that other generalizations which are not much more defensible are often taken seriously. For example, young learners may make generalizations such as:

A. Teachers are kind. I know because both of my teachers have been kind to me.

  B.   Collie dogs are good-natured. My collie has never bitten anyone.

  C.   Stepmothers are mean. Snow White's stepmother was, and so are the ones on television.

  D.   People from that part of town are lazy. Johnny Jones is from that part of town, and he never works.

When we encounter such assertions in classrooms we need to help learners examine them intelligently. This examination might begin by raising, in an appropriate way, issues such as: (1) Is the statement based on relevant evidence? and (2) Is there sufficient evidence to justify tentative acceptance of the statement? In the examples above the learners do have, from their own experience, evidence which seems to support the generalizations. The problem is that the evidence is not sufficient. Learners can be helped to recognize this by being encouraged to raise a third very important question: What do we do when we encounter more evidence? This question is important because any generalization made on the basis of a *sample* of evidence is tentative and hence may be disconfirmed by new evidence. A generalization should not be used to categorize new members of the set. Thus, in the above examples, the young learners should be encouraged to:

  A.   View a new teacher as evidence to test the generalization "Teachers are kind." Since the generalization is accepted only tentatively, it would be a mistake to say of the new teacher, "This person is kind because he is a teacher, and teachers are kind."

B. See another collie dog as evidence to test the generalization, "Collie dogs are good-natured."

C. Treat additional stepmothers as opportunities to test the assertion, "Stepmothers are mean."

D. View persons from "that part of town" as an opportunity to test the generalization, "People from that part of town are lazy."

In short, learners need to become aware that most generalizations are tentative; hence, new evidence should be viewed as a chance to test the generalization. Critical thinking is obstructed when generalizations are held as certain and are used to categorize unexamined members of the class or set in question. Such categorization encourages prejudice and discourages critical thought. In making a generalization our job is to gather as much evidence as is possible and feasible prior to drawing the generalization. Once we have made the generalization we need to remind ourselves and learners that it is properly viewed as if it were preceded by the phrase, "We have reason to believe that . . . ," and followed by, ". . . although we could be wrong."

In the classroom there are many opportunities to encourage learners to improve their critical-thinking ability by improving their ability to make and evaluate generalizations. One starting point might be the learners' generalizations based upon evidence which may be insufficient—e.g.:

Policemen are mean.

Dogs and cats are natural enemies.

People without jobs are lazy.

The Chinese can't be trusted.

Women are terrible drivers.

When a generalization of this kind is made in a classroom, learners should be encouraged to examine the evidence on which it is based. Such examination may cause learners to reject the generalization on the grounds that the evidence is not sufficient. Or they may find new evidence which refutes the generalization. And in some cases they may find evidence which gives further support to the generalization. But in any case, learners should be aided in developing an open attitude and a willingness to test their own generalizations as new evidence becomes available. They can then come to understand that whether a generalization is justified is primarily a question of evidence. Hence, one may be justified in holding a generalization today which may need modification tomorrow when new evidence appears.

Critical Thinking and Settlement of Disputes

The major purpose of this chapter is to look at some skills which learners may acquire to help them settle intelligently certain kinds of debates or disputes which occur in and out of classrooms. We hear a great deal these days about disagreement, dissent, and dispute. It is often pointed out that the clash of opposing views is to be welcomed, for many good ideas are the product of intelligent and forceful dissent. This is true, and its importance for teaching is great indeed. To have as a primary purpose the development of thinking persons is to demand that disagreement and dispute be welcomed in the classroom. But to say that opposing views on virtually any question should be welcomed in the classroom does not mean that all views are equally sound or that any view should go unchallenged.

We might agree that every person has a right to his own opinion, but we certainly would not agree that simply because an opinion is one's own it is therefore good. Given any conflict of opinions or any set of opposing views, learners should be encouraged to ask whether the dispute, if important, can be intelligently settled. Now, some can and some can't. All disputes can, however, be thoughtfully examined. Such an examination should allow learners to identify those conflicts which can be intelligently resolved and the procedures which would be necessary to bring the resolution about.

THREE KINDS OF DISPUTES

Disputes can be categorized in many different ways. One way is to use categories that reflect the kinds of claims which are disputed. Such categories are useful because different kinds of claims require different kinds of evaluation. But what do we mean by "different kinds of claims"?

A. All spinsters in Brooklyn are unmarried.

B. Water freezes at temperatures below 32° F.

C. $2 + 2 = 4$.

D. The capital of California is Sacramento.

Each of the above is a "claim," and we would probably agree that these claims are true. But what if someone said that they were *not* true? If we were in doubt—if there was a dispute about the truth of these claims—how should we go about removing that doubt? Let's begin with claim "A." If we were to ask someone to "find out" if "A" is true, it seems likely that he would say that he doesn't have to find out—that claim "A" is true by definition. And this in a sense is a correct answer. One does not have to go to Brooklyn to survey spinsters or go through court records. One finds out by simply analyzing the language of the claim. Nothing one might find in Brooklyn could make the claim false. The claim is "analytically," or "logically," true: We can determine its truth using the rules of logic or mathematics.

Are there any other of our sample claims which are analytic? Yes, statement "C," "2 + 2 = 4." This is a mathematical claim: It is true in the "game" of elementary arithmetic. One does not have to go out into the world and count "things" to know that this claim is true, for its truth is determined by appeal to the "rules of the game." The game in this case is not language or logic but arithmetic.

What about claims "B" and "D"? What would we do if someone asked us how we *know* that these are true? Clearly we cannot demonstrate the truth of such claims by appealing to the rules of language and logic. We might say that we would *show* the doubter. *What* we would show him would be evidence. In the case of the capital of California we might go to the geography book. If the doubter still doubted, we might suggest he go to California and find out for himself. In the case of the water we might first refer the one who doubted to a science book. Or, if we have the opportunity, we might ask that he test this himself: that he place some water in temperatures below 32° F. and see what happens. But what's the point of all this? It is simply that this is a different category of claim calling for a different method of evaluation or verification. Claims like "B" and "D" are called "empirical claims." An empirical claim is one which purports to describe something in our world of experience. Such a claim can be verified only by looking at that world—i.e., empirical claims can be verified only with empirical evidence. There are no rules of language, logic, or mathematics that will guarantee the truth of an empirical claim. Thus, when we encounter a dispute about empirical matter we should recognize that it can be settled intelligently only by examining the appropriate empirical evidence.

There is a third and very important category of dispute which we will mention briefly here and will treat in some detail in the next chapter. This is the value dispute. A value claim is one which assigns value to some object or act. Examples of value claims are:

E. It is good to be honest.

F. One should seek pleasure and avoid pain.

Some disputes which appear to be about matters of value can be resolved by logical argument or empirical evidence. In other cases, however, value disputes seem to defy rational resolution. We will talk about the justification of value statements in the next chapter. For the present time, let us simply note that there are such disputes, that they occur frequently in classrooms, and that very often they cannot be settled in the same way as analytic and empirical claims.

CLAIMS AND CASES

When we want to examine the worth of a claim we have made, or when we want to make a judgment about a claim made by someone else, how should we go about it? We might ask *why* we should believe the claim, or we might ask the person making the claim to demonstrate that it is true. To put this another way, we might well ask the person making the claim to explain his *grounds* for the claim, or what he takes to be adequate support for his claim. Thus, to make a judgment about a claim we ask for the "supporting case" for the claim. Hence, to evaluate a claim we need to know both what the case is and what kind of case would be required to provide adequate support for the claim.

Of course claims may be made, either by us or by others, without having *any* case to support them. When we find that this has occurred, what we have is a claim which is unsupported by the person making it. This does not, of course, mean that the claim is false. It might well be true. In such an instance our judgment might be that the person making the claim is in no position to really *know* that it is true (or false), since he does not know the case which would demonstrate that truth. The claim is unsupported. The judgment of truth or falsity can be made only after the case has been built and examined.

Our major point here is that in order to evaluate a claim we must examine the case which is held to support the claim. In order to evaluate a case for any claim, we must know what kind of claim is being made and what sort of case is required. In the preceding section we talked about different kinds of claims. Let us now turn to an examination of the cases required to support those claims.

Empirical cases.   We have already seen that we determine the truth or falsity of an empirical claim *only* by looking to the appropriate empirical evidence. The case for an empirical claim is a report of the relevant empirical evidence. To evaluate the empirical case we would ask questions such as:

(a)   Is the evidence offered in the case relevant; i.e., does the evidence support the claim?

(b) Is the evidence offered sufficient; i.e., is there enough evidence to warrant our believing that the claim is true?

Now, this may seem like common sense hardly worth repeating, but learners need to develop the skills of recognizing empirical claims and examining and judging evidential cases which are offered in support of those claims. Classrooms abound with opportunities to exercise these skills. But there are also some general kinds of problems which learners are likely to encounter as they practice evaluating empirical claims and cases. Let us look at some of the more common of these problems.

A learner often makes an empirical claim on the basis of very scanty evidence or no evidence at all. If asked for his case, he may reply, "It's just what I *think*." How should we respond to this in order to aid learners in developing skills of critical thinking? Clearly we want them to feel free to report their guesses, hunches, assumptions, etc. But we should also work to help them see that the hunch or guess is *not* a case: The case is the evidence we use to test the hunches or guesses. Thus, learners need to come to see that we can evaluate an empirical claim only with an empirical case. When an empirical claim is made without a case, we look at the evidence to test the claim. Or to put this in a different way, the empirical claim without a case is an unverified hypothesis. The hypothesis is tested by looking to the appropriate empirical evidence.

Sometimes empirical claims are made but cannot be verified. This occurs when we have no evidence or very little evidence. For example, suppose an argument develops in an elementary classroom about life on other planets. One learner says that there are intelligent beings on other planets. A second learner disagrees. Now, this is an empirical disagreement, and one about which we cannot at present gather empirical evidence to build a strong evidential case for either of the claims. What we *can* agree about is what would count as evidence *and* the fact that we do not have that evidence. It may be that our learners will continue to debate the question, but until further evidence becomes available the debate seems fruitless. The case required is an empirical one, and it is only with an empirical case that the issue can be resolved. What the learners have in this dispute are hypotheses. Each may feel very strongly about his hypothesis, but strength of feeling is no substitute for evidence. With respect to these competing claims or hypotheses, verification or "settlement" is not possible at present. With such questions we should perhaps recognize that the most reasonable course of action is to suspend judgment; to conclude that the evidence at this time is too sketchy to warrant strong belief in either of the propositions.

There is not, of course, a sharp line which separates adequate from inadequate evidence for an empirical claim. Suppose a learner were to assert that most fifth-graders are more interested in reading adventure stories than biographies. When asked for his evidence or "case," he explains that he has asked his classmates and has found this to be true. How good is his evidence? We might say that his claim is too broad, that his evidence gives strong support to the more limited claim that most of his classmates are more interested in adventure stories. But what of his original assertion? His evidence gives *some* support to it, but certainly not conclusive support. Here again we find that the generalization is based on or supported by very sketchy evidence. If our learner examines the case for the claim—the evidence which would resolve a dispute about the claim—he will discover that the case is weak. This does not mean that he should dismiss the claim as false. It does mean that he should recognize the limitations of the evidence, that the evidential case is so weak that perhaps he should suspend judgment until more information can be gathered.

Focusing on evidence as a way to settle empirical disputes is important, but in some cases there are misleading appeals to evidence. One such misleading appeal is the "selective" use of evidence. Learners need to recognize that the case for an empirical claim must take into account *all* of the relevant evidence available rather than simply selecting that part of the evidence which supports the claim. Suppose that in discussing automobile safety a learner asserts that women drivers have more automobile accidents than do men. To support his claim he lists as evidence the facts that several of his friends' mothers have been involved in auto accidents, that he has observed several accidents involving women drivers, and so forth. He does not, until asked, furnish the information that several of his friends' fathers have also had accidents or that in the accidents he has observed many have involved male as well as female drivers. In short, this learner may correctly see his claim as one which requires empirical evidence, but he may pick from the total evidence which is available only that which lends support to his claim. This may be a useful technique in debating, but it misleads us when we attempt to evaluate a claim. A case for an empirical claim must include all the relevant evidence we have, not just that part of the evidence which pleases us or which supports a claim we want supported.

In summary, an empirical claim is evaluated by looking at the empirical evidence. The empirical evidence is the case required to resolve an empirical dispute. In classrooms we often find empirical claims made without a case being offered. Until we can examine the case we cannot make a judgment about the claim. Another problem encountered in the classroom is the empirical claim for which no evidence or very little evidence is available. Such a claim simply cannot be settled until the evidence becomes available. A third problem which may appear is that learners may "build" empirical cases for their claims by ignoring some of the relevant evidence. This is misleading, since the case can be used for evaluation of the claim only if it includes *all* of the relevant evidence which is available. Our basic concern in this section is that learners need to be helped to develop skill in recognizing empirical claims and evaluating the evidential cases offered in support of those claims.

Logical cases. Some "analytic" or "logical" claims contain within themselves all the case needed for evaluation. The term "tautology" is sometimes used to describe such claims. One example of a tautology used previously is, "All spinsters in Brooklyn are unmarried." A quick examination of the words used in this claim shows that it is true, for its truth rests not on what happens in Brooklyn but on the way we use the word "spinster." There are many statements of this sort, statements which are true simply because of the language used. A common mistake made with respect to such claims is the assumption that they contain empirical information. They do not. They tell us nothing about the empirical world, and nothing we could find in the empirical world—Brooklyn in this example—could be counted as relevant evidence.

Just as some claims are analytically or logically true, others are logically false. If someone were to say that there was indeed a spinster in Brooklyn who was happily married, we could say that the claim was false. If a woman is a spinster she is unmarried; if she is married she is not a spinster. And, again, no matter what happens in Brooklyn the claim is false. It is a matter of language and logic that to be a spinster is to be unmarried. It is not a claim which requires empirical evidence.

Not all analytic claims contain within themselves the case necessary for deciding if they are true or false. In many instances the claim is but a conclusion, and the case needed to support that conclusion is a logical argument. In the case of a conclusion in mathematics we recognize the importance of the "case," or use of the rules of mathematics, in arriving at the conclusion. But we often overlook the importance of building a logical case for a logical conclusion. We discussed earlier several common logical fallacies and some common valid argument forms. Fallacies can be regarded as faulty logical cases. A sound case must follow a valid argument form.

Wrong cases. If learners develop skill in distinguishing between logical and empirical claims and in recognizing the kind of case which is required to resolve each, they will avoid two very common and very serious errors in evaluating claims. One such error is to give an empirical case in support of a logical claim.

The other is to offer a logical case in defense of an empirical claim.

In the case of the first error, if we sent someone to Brooklyn to run a survey to find out if the spinsters there are indeed unmarried, we would be gathering empirical evidence to test a claim which is logically true. And not only is such an empirical test unnecessary, it is irrelevant. The researcher in Brooklyn might find many interesting things, but nothing he could find challenges the truth of the logical claim. Even so, this error probably causes much less difficulty than does the second.

The error of offering a logical argument as evidence of the truth of an empirical claim often gets in the way of resolving disputes. Notice the following common claims which are made about teaching:

(a) Children will achieve better when grouped according to ability than when placed in heterogeneous groups.

(b) Teachers who have themselves come from "culturally disadvantaged" backgrounds will work better with children from such backgrounds than will teachers from "middle class" backgrounds.

(c) Children can't learn in a noisy classroom.

(d) If we were to double the pay given teachers, they would become more devoted to the task of helping children learn.

Each of the above is an empirical claim. Each is also a claim likely to be debated as if truth or falsity could be determined by logical argument. Often one hears in such debates statements such as, "It only stands to reason that . . . ," or, "It's only common sense that . . ." But reason and/or common sense do not make a case either *for* or *against* any of these claims. Common sense or reason may furnish us with hypotheses, but the case needed to resolve a dispute about these claims is an empirical one. The claims can be verified or rejected only with empirical evidence. To argue about these claims as if persuasion rather than empirical evidence is the important thing is to waste one's time. And we might note in passing that there is not conclusive evidence for the truth of any one of these sample claims.

SUMMARY

One goal of critical thinking is to resolve intelligently those disputes which can be so resolved. Learners need to develop skills which will allow them to identify the different sorts of claims which may be disputed and to know the appropriate way to go about intelligent resolution. Three basic kinds of claims are (a) empirical, (b) logical, and (c) value. To resolve a dispute about a claim, one must look at the appropriate case for the claim.

Critical Thinking and Value Judgments

In the preceding chapter our concern was with critical thinking as a means to resolve empirical and logical disputes. This is an important matter, and it is with such disputes that we can most easily demonstrate the importance of some skills in critical thinking. Learners may see as problematic questions such as whether a certain mathematical problem is worked correctly, or if the area of the school gymnasium is greater than the area of the combined academic classrooms, or whether novelists earn as much money as physicians, or whether agricultural production in Latin America is rising or falling. With such questions we know the kind of case we would need to support an answer, and we know how to evaluate cases which are given. If we have the evidence or the rules, we can then resolve many disputes which arise. However, even when logical and empirical disagreements are settled, new problems and disputes may arise. Learners may, for example, raise questions such as:

Should the gymnasium of a school have an area greater than the combined areas of academic classrooms?

Ought novelists' incomes to compare favorably with that of physicians?

Should the goal in Latin American agriculture be increased production?

In attempting to answer such questions empirical evidence is important. In the case of the first question, if it is true that the academic classroom activities require less space than do the physical education and entertainment activities, that fact should be taken into account when we make our decision. In the third example, the fact that many Latin American people suffer from malnutrition is relevant information. Yet such facts, though important, are not sufficient grounds on which to base a conclusion. The questions call for judgments of value.

In answering value questions our concern is not merely with asserting that something is the case (e.g., Latin Americans suffer from malnutrition because of insufficient food). We want to say as well that something is good or bad, worthy or unworthy. When someone else assigns a *different* value to the same act or object, we say we have a value conflict. And value conflicts, we all know, are not easily resolved. Because we do often disagree about matters of value and because such disagreements are not easily settled, we are tempted to try to avoid dealing with "controversial" value disputes in our classrooms. Value disputes, some argue, do not lend themselves to rigorous and thoughtful examination and evaluation.

It is not surprising that this position is sometimes taken by teachers. It does appear that our conflict-resolving apparatus breaks down when we confront a value disagreement. Some value disagreements have been with us through the ages, and our inability to reach agreement is clear to us all. And because we cannot, or at least do not, agree, we are tempted to exclude value questions from those things to which we apply the tools of critical thinking. Thus, we may leave valuing to be done on the basis of feeling, desire, instinct, or whim.

This rejection of critical thinking as a means to settle value matters or value disputes is reflected in the popular quip, "One person's opinion is as good as another's." Now, in some areas and at some times we may wish to hold to this view of the equal worth of opinions, but these areas and times need to be carefully specified so that we do not reject necessary inquiry. It is clear that such a view would be nonsensical if it were held to be true of questions of fact: One person's opinion on a factual matter is as good as another's only if both are in accordance with the facts or both are in error. But of course our concern here is not with facts but with values. Is it true that any opinion about a matter of value is of equal worth with any other opinion? Most of us would probably say "no" if we were asked such questions as:

Is the view that killing another human being is usually justifiable as good as the opinion that such killing is seldom justifiable?

Is a propensity for dishonesty as good as a propensity for honesty?

Is approval of cruelty to other human beings as good as disapproval?

The vast majority of us would refuse vehemently to answer these questions affirmatively. This, of course, would not mean that we are right and all others are wrong, but it does suggest that when we are faced with some extreme stands on moral issues we depart from the view that all opinions are of equal worth. Although we want learners to become tolerant (this in itself reflects a value), we do not want them to believe that their values make no difference or that any set of values is as good as any other. In short, we are as concerned with the "valuing" students do as well as with their "knowing." But what can and should schools do with respect to their students' values? Is there any role to be played by critical thinking?

Traditionally, our answer to the problem of "value education" has been concerned more with informing learners, of giving them knowledge than with working with them to develop skill in solving value problems. Or to put this another way, we sometimes attempt to meet the need for value education by teaching learners moral rules: e.g., one should not steal; honesty is the best policy; it is wrong to harm another person. The assumption has seemed to be that when learners have mastered enough of these rules, we have succeeded at the task of "moral" or "ethical" or "value" education. It is as if we believed that learners, when armed with such rules, were ready to face life with ready-made "good" decisions.

Of course we don't really believe this. We know that there may be serious disagreement as to what qualifies as "moral knowledge" or a "rule." Even if we agree on the rules, we know that many such rules, if not all, have exceptions. Thus, we might hold that "Honesty is the best policy" is not an absolute rule, but is rather a kind of rule of thumb appropriate in *most* cases. There are some contexts, we might argue, in which the moral thing to do is *not* to tell the truth. For example, we might insist that it would be right not to tell the truth to a homicidal maniac, in order to keep him from killing or hurting an innocent person. In admitting that there may be disagreement as to what the moral rules are, or that there may be exceptions to the rules we accept, we are in effect saying that the "transmitted knowledge" view is at best incomplete. If there are exceptions to the rules, then learners must decide when the rule should be applied and when it should be ignored. How are learners to be prepared to deal with these exceptions? How are they to know if a situation calls for behavior specified by the rule, or if it is a case which is an exception?

Some would say that these questions simply accentuate the point that value judgments are a matter of individual preference. But there is an alternative. The fact that our moral rules admit of exceptions can be taken as reason to pay more attention rather than less to giving learners practice in using skills of critical thinking in making value judgments. Our concern as teachers should be to help learners develop the ability to *do* something (value intelligently) rather than simply learn a set of rules. But what does it mean to value intelligently? This is of course the central question, and we will now look at some tentative and partial answers to that question.

VALUE CLAIMS AND VALUE CASES

To say that critical thinking is appropriate in the making and evaluating of value claims is to say in effect that cases can be made for value claims just as they can for empirical or logical claims. Our task here, then, is to ask what a "good case" for a value claim would be. To answer this question we will look at three different kinds of statements which are often called "value statements" or "value judgments" in the classroom.

Preference Claims. One of the reasons for our tendency to say that it makes no sense to argue about values is that we sometimes use the term "value judgment" or "value statement" to refer to a person's statement of preference. The following are some examples of preference statements:

I like to play baseball.

I prefer art class to music class.

I do not like to study history.
I would rather dig ditches than do long division.

We often refer to such statements as value statements. Now, it is not our job here to tell people what they should call things, but it is necessary to point out that the above preference statements are quite different from what are here called value statements. A value claim is one which assigns or attributes value to some act or object. These preference claims, on the other hand, simply report what some person likes or dislikes, approves or disapproves. You like to work long division problems, and I don't. I like Chinese food, and you don't. These are differences in preferences, not values. When you claim to like to struggle with long division and I claim to be addicted to Chinese food, we have made claims about ourselves, not about long division or Chinese food.

What sort of case is needed to support a preference claim? This is where the business of "to each his own" makes a good deal of sense. When we are speaking of our preferences, our likes and dislikes, we often do not require any case. We simply take the person's word about his preferences. But even if you don't want to take my word about my taste for Chinese food, the case you would look for would not require that you examine the merits of Chinese food: You would look at my behavior. If you observed that I studiously avoid Chinese restaurants, you might claim to have a case to support the claim that I do not relish Chinese food. In most cases, however, when we are dealing with preferences we don't worry about cases: We simply agree to disagree. Certainly it would be absurd to spend large amounts of school time to "debate" values when there is no basis for debate. The fact that you like to work long-division problems and I don't provides no grounds for debate. We may very well agree as to what long division is and what can be done with it. We also agree that you like it and I don't. There is, then, no disagreement about long division—there are merely different preferences with respect to it.

The distinction between value and preference statements is useful, since preference statements generally require no case, and hence we are seldom seriously concerned with resolving a "dispute" about them. Sometimes, however, one must examine a statement carefully in order to decide whether it is a value or a preference claim. Quite often a claim is made that *looks* like a value claim when, in fact, the person making the statement is only reporting his preferences. Notice the following value claims:

Novelists ought to be paid as much as physicians.

That was a good television drama.

Coed schools are better than noncoed schools.

In many contexts these would indeed be value claims. In some cases, however, they may be intended as reports of preferences. Suppose we asked for the case which the person would use to support the claim that the television drama was a good one, and the person replied that what he meant was that he *liked* the show, or that he would much rather watch *that* show than the late weather report. His "case" is merely his preference, a claim about himself, and not a claim about the television show. Again, we would not want to spend much time debating whether this *was* his preference. And the question of whether he *should* prefer what he does in fact prefer is a question of a different order. The point here is quite simple: Some statements which are of the *form* of value statements turn out to be simply statements of preference. Because preference statements are claims about the person making the statement and *not* value claims regarding that which is preferred, they seldom present "disputes" which call for resolution.

Value-empirical Claims. Just as some statements having the form of value claims are really statements of preference, so are some other statements which take the form of value statements actually empirical claims. When we encounter a statement of the latter sort we sometimes treat it as a value question which we do not know how to resolve rather than an empirical question which we do know how to settle. For example, suppose that the following argument occurred in a faculty room:

Teacher A: A quiet classroom is a good classroom. Children ought to be required to be quiet while in school.

Teacher B: I disagree. I don't think that a good classroom is necessarily a quiet one. And I don't think that we should require children to be quiet in school.

Teacher C: It's all a matter of personal opinion. You have each given your value judgments, and it's foolish to argue.

What should we say of such an argument? Right away we should be suspicious of what Teacher *C* has said. But let us start with Teachers *A* and *B*. Suppose we asked them for the "cases" for their claims, and received the following responses:

Teacher A: A quiet classroom is a good classroom because it promotes learning. Children ought to be required to be quiet while in school because they will then learn more.

Teacher B: A quiet classroom is not necessarily a good classroom, because very often keeping children quiet does not promote learning in the classroom. Hence, there should be no requirement that children be quiet while in school.

What do these cases suggest? Teacher *A* and Teacher *B* agree that learning should be promoted. What they disagree about is the means to be used. What sort of classroom atmosphere best promotes learning? This is the question, and it is one which is neither a

question of value nor a question of logic. It is an empirical question. The claim of Teacher *A* could be summarized thus: "If a classroom is quiet, children will
learn more." The claim Teacher *B* has made is a de-
nial of the claim made by Teacher *A*. The dispute is
one which can be settled with empirical evidence and
only with empirical evidence. Of course, it is possible
that the evidence will show that Teacher *A*'s students
learn more in a quiet classroom, and Teacher *B*'s in a
room that is not so quiet. But in any case, logical argument will not settle the matter, and it would be sense-
less to regard the dispute as one about values even
though the statements may take the form of value
statements. In the original argument, Teachers *A* and
B may or may not understand the nature of their dispute. Teacher *C* clearly does not.

Again our point is a simple one. Many statements
which take the form of value claims are in fact empirical claims. Teachers can help learners to recognize
these statements for what they are and, once recognized, to treat them as any other empirical claim. Such
claims can often be easily recognized by the "case" or
reason given. When the case or reason for some
"value" is that what is valued will lead to something
else, what we have is an empirical claim. The following are some further examples of "value claims" which
are in fact empirical claims:

1. (a) *apparent value claim:* You ought not to cheat on
examinations. The reason for this is that such cheating
leads to severe punishment.

(b) *masquerading empirical claim:* If you cheat on
examinations, you will be punished severely.

2. (a) *apparent value claim:* We should all be honest with others, for they will then be honest with us.

(b) *masquerading empirical claim:* If we are honest with others, they will be honest with us.

3. (a) *apparent value claim:* Black coffee is good. I say this because it keeps me awake.

(b) *masquerading empirical claim:* If I drink black coffee, I stay awake.

Thus, some disputes which may appear to be value conflicts turn out to be disputes about matters of empirical fact. And clearly such disputes belong in classrooms, not to be debated on logical grounds but as hypotheses to be tested with empirical evidence.

Value claims and value conflicts. We have now shown that some claims which look like value claims are really preference statements. Others have been seen to be claims about matters of empirical fact. But we finally have to face the issue. There are claims which *are* value claims and which cannot be disregarded as easily as preference claims. Nor can real value conflicts be resolved as easily as can a disagreement about the truth of an empirical claim. Using one of our earlier examples, suppose we encounter the claim that we should be honest with others. Suppose further that when we ask *why* we should be honest—when we ask for the case of the claim—the person answers that this is the moral thing to do, that a society in which men follow this maxim is a better society. Moreover, the person making the claim insists that he is not just telling us what he likes or prefers, nor is he making an empirical claim, although both his preferences and some empirical claims may be a part of the case he is making. He is attempting to justify his assignment of value, to give his reasons (and the appropriate empirical evidence) for assigning value as he does. His reasons may be good or bad. The point here is only that his *reasons* for holding a value position become his case for that position.

Such a value case can be examined using skills of critical thinking. This does not mean that thoughtful examination will resolve all value disputes. But such examination will show *some* cases to be faulty. And by showing strengths and weaknesses of various value cases we may resolve some value conflicts; i.e., by examining "cases" for value claims with the persons making those claims, some value conflicts are resolvable. Not all value conflicts will be resolved in this way. Different and conflicting value positions may be held and may be equally "justified" by their holders. Value conflicts are sometimes real. Critical thinking can be used to separate the real conflicts from pseudo conflicts.

Let us look at an example of how we might examine a case for a value claim. Suppose one of our fellow teachers asserts that all teachers should feel obliged to join professional organizations because such joining indicates that teachers are professional people. We then ask him why teachers should be professional people. Of course there are all sorts of answers to this question, but let us assume that our colleague will be cooperative in providing us with a suitable answer for our purposes here—let us assume that he responds by saying that it is simply good to be professional, *just because*. He is thus assigning value, not making an empirical claim. How might we go about examining or thinking through such a value position? One thing we would want to do is to examine the reasons he offers. Do we accept those reasons? If among his reasons are some empirical claims, are those claims true? Is he, and are we, willing to accept the logical conclusions of his reasons? Following this sort of examination, we might then look at alternative value positions and alternative reasons. Thus, if our colleague insists that every teacher should join professional organizations, we might ask him questions such as the following:

(1) If the teacher has good reason to believe that the professional organization is corrupt, should he join nevertheless?

(2) If membership in the organization would require so much of the teacher's time that he could not do an adequate job of teaching, would it still be "good" to join?

(3) If the professional organization is seen to function contrary to the best interests of the society, should the teacher join?

The list of questions could be greatly extended. If such questions are taken seriously, they will help to clarify the case for the value statement and make it easier for both our colleague and ourselves to evaluate the case and the claim. Our colleague may, for example, wish to modify his claim somewhat as follows:

As a teacher one ought to be professional. This is indicated by membership in professional organizations which one believes are not corrupt, which will not prevent the teacher from doing an adequate job in the classroom, which do not function contrary to the best interests of the society, etc.

With each modification made, the value claim and the case for the claim become more clear. This does not mean that we will agree with our colleague. We may find a contrary claim and case more appealing. Hence, even after our examination there may be a value conflict. But the examination may allow us to avoid the pseudo conflicts, to understand what the real conflict is and what the competing cases for competing value decisions are.

SUMMARY

Critical thinking can and should be used in examining questions and claims of value. Some disputes commonly referred to as "value conflicts" are not really value conflicts but are rather differences in preferences or disagreements about matters of empirical fact. Learners need to be helped in developing the skills to recognize these pseudo-value conflicts. But there are *real* value claims and value conflicts. Cases for value claims can and should be examined in classrooms. Not all value conflicts will disappear on examination, but the examination will clarify what the dispute is and what the cases are for the competing claims. It is perhaps at this point—after critical examination—that learners should be encouraged to agree to disagree. "One person's opinion is as good as another's" may simply mean that well-informed and thoughtful people do in fact often disagree. But that fact should not encourage us to avoid value problems in the classroom. Helping learners to become well-informed and thoughtful about matters of value, not simply getting them to agree, is the important goal of the teacher who wants to encourage critical thinking.

Reading and Thinking

Throughout this book we have emphasized the importance of helping learners develop skills of critical thinking, or problem-solving. The position taken has been that these skills are best developed through practice, and that opportunities for such practice are present in every subject-matter field. There is an assumption which underlies this position. That assumption is that problem-solving ability is the crucial human characteristic, the characteristic which allows us to gain increased control over our environment and ourselves, and thus gives us the potential to improve the quality of our lives. How are learners to understand and examine this assumption? How are they to come to see that problem-solving is not simply a school exercise but is both very common and extremely important in everyone's life? Developing the skills of critical thinking is not enough: We must also work to develop attitudes about that thinking.

We all know that simply telling learners that something is important is not very effective. We must help them discover for themselves that critical thinking is important for men and societies in general, and for each of them in particular. There is no magic formula we can use to guarantee that the young will make this discovery. We can, however, encourage them to examine their own experiences, both direct and vicarious, to find out how critical thinking, or the lack of critical thinking, has affected their lives and the lives of others. What sorts of experiences could be used for this purpose? The answer is: nearly *all* of the learners' experiences. But there is a particular kind of vicarious experience which we will emphasize in this chapter, both because it can be dealt with easily and naturally in schools and because it provides clear and compelling examples of the importance of problem-solving in the lives of men. This experience is reading. Books provide a rich and varied resource in man's attempts to solve the problems he faces.

Every teacher sometimes asks learners to think about what they are reading. However, most of us seldom emphasize to learners that, even with their so-called "free reading," much of their reading is reading *about* thinking. This is true whether they are reading fiction or nonfiction. Books are, after all, the primary place to find the thinking process recorded. And if we want to check our own thinking on a given topic or problem, books are a primary source we use to find what others have thought on the same topic. Not only are the thoughts of "Greats" to be found in books, but so are the thoughts of ordinary people in ordinary situations. Many children's books, for example, deal with the way in which children have solved or failed to solve problems facing them. There is no reason, of course, to believe that reading *about* thinking will improve learners' skills of critical thinking, but such reading can be utilized by the teacher to help learners come to see how important, and how common, problem-solving is in the life of every person.

If we look at the books children read—books they read because they enjoy them and not simply because they are told to read—we find illustrations of many of the skills discussed in this book. In these books, both fiction and nonfiction, we find accounts of how persons have gone about the business of solving problems. Some of the problems are important, some unimportant; some are simple, others are complex. And some of the attempts to solve problems are intelligent, others unintelligent; some are successful while others fail. But in any case, we find our underlying assumption reflected in many books: If people develop and exercise their potential for critical thinking, they thereby increase their control over themselves and their environment. In discussing with learners the books they read, we can help them recognize the role played by critical thought in their own lives as well as in those lives they read about.

To illustrate how children's books do reflect an emphasis on the importance of critical thinking, we will now look at some passages from a number of these books.[1] The books discussed in the following pages cover a wide range of topics and reading levels.

CRITICAL THINKING IN NONFICTION BOOKS FOR CHILDREN

Learners are often fascinated by accounts of the great men in human history, men who have played significant roles in altering the course of our history. Many lessons can be learned by studying the lives of such men, and one such lesson must be that these men have had the ability to recognize problems in the world around them and the courage to attempt to find

[1] The books discussed in this chapter were furnished by the Books for Young Readers division of Doubleday. No attempt has been made to examine or evaluate other children's books which are readily available for classroom use.

solutions for those problems. These men are also favorite subjects for authors to write about; hence, there is no shortage of books about great men in history.

One of the greatest "problem-solvers" in the history of Western civilization is Leonardo da Vinci. The spirit and content of Da Vinci's thought have been captured for the young reader in Richard McLanathan's *Images of the Universe: Leonardo da Vinci: —The Artist as Scientist.* In the Introduction of this book, Professor Abbott Payson Usher says of Da Vinci, "Throughout his life his mind was constantly turning from one problem to another." And indeed this is what is shown in the book. One can look at almost any page and find an example of how Da Vinci recognized and sought to solve a problem that was facing mankind. As an example, the following section gives an indication not only of the power of his thought but also the impact of that thought on our history:

The use of a falling weight as a source of power came to be so completely associated with clocks that it has been considered a purely clockwork mechanism from the later Middle Ages on. But Leonardo, as we have seen, applied it to all sorts of other devices, including his file cutter, in which the aim of automation is clear, since the mechanism was designed to complete each file without the need of an operator. Though there is no record that such a machine was ever constructed, its principle is sound and workable, and a single person could keep a dozen or more machines in constant production.

He also experimented with another source of power closely associated with clocks since the sixteenth century, the spring. He conjectured using springs to drive a curious self-propelled vehicle he designed, and they also appear as an assistance to manpower in a drawing for one of his many schemes for a flying machine.

The idea embodied in his file cutter, of economy of manpower and standardization of the process, and consequently of the product, was not realized until centuries after Leonardo's day, but his notes and sketches are full of it. His nap-raising machine, for example, could handle five widths of material at once, and his shearing machine four, while his needle grinder was to finish 400 needles in an hour. In his drawings for the various machines to produce coinage for the papal mint, he devised automatic hammers working off a central power source so that eight machines could be in simultaneous controlled production of the metal bars from which coin blanks were stamped. His milling machine was planned to bridge a canalized river with several undershot wheels driving a multiple-unit mill on both sides of the stream. Here, as in so many other of his schemes, the far-reaching implications are of infinitely greater importance than the immediate application, for Leonardo, intensely practical though he was, has an even more significant place as a pioneer in new conceptions than as an inventor of individual devices.

When machines were made individually, each for a separate job, there could be no hope for the standardization necessary to realize Leonardo's revolutionary ideal. It was not until the eighteenth century that mass production was finally achieved through the use of interchangeable parts: In 1765 a French artillery general named Gribeauval produced a number of gun carriages in this way. And in 1784 Thomas Jefferson reported from Paris that he had seen musket locks similarly made. It remained for a Connecticut Yankee named Eli Whitney, the inventor of the cotton gin, to develop the method, considered impossible by leading European military experts, in his production of rifles for the United States Government. Another Connecticut man, Eli Terry, applied the same idea to the manufacture of clocks. Sewing machines and agricultural equipment followed. The machine-tool industry was in full swing. And the machine-centered modern world, with its ever increasing production, was born, and developing automation, as Leonardo had envisioned, began freeing man from the burden of the centuries, slavery to manual labor, with results so revolutionary that we have not yet been able to understand or control them.[2]

Even this brief passage makes clear the impact of a single man's thought on human history. It also shows that finding solutions for particular problems does not make it less necessary for men in succeeding generations to develop skills of critical thinking. Da Vinci's principles of mass production have, in the last two centuries, been used to solve some problems, but these solutions have created new problems. The need for problem-solving is a continuing and expanding one.

Not all great men are as well-known as Da Vinci. The history of the United States furnishes many examples of men who were great in the sense that they faced crucial problems and worked intelligently but against great odds to solve them. Some of the most striking cases are found in the rise of the Negro from slavery. In *Four Took Freedom*, Philip Sterling and Rayford Logan describe the lives of four American Negroes who escaped from slavery and dedicated their lives to the problem of improving America by improving the lot of the American Negro. The four are Harriet Tubman, Frederick Douglass, Robert Smalls, and Blanche K. Bruce. This book makes clear that these were extremely courageous Americans. It also demonstrates that they were highly creative and intelligent problem-solvers, and that is our interest here.

[2] Richard McLanathan, *Images of the Universe*, p. 151.

Let us take Robert Smalls as a case in point. When Smalls escaped, he did so by taking over a Confederate ship which he then turned over to the Union Navy:

Every wind that blew from Port Royal carried the scent of freedom, and Robert Smalls took deeper breaths from day to day. He had to talk to Hannah.

"There must be some way to get to Port Royal."

"Roads full of patrollers," Hannah replied. "Woods full of soldiers and rivers full of picket boats. You're talking foolishness, man."

"I'm thinking of sailing to Port Royal in the *Planter.*"

Hannah shook her head disbelievingly. "How you gonna get me and the children on board? And what about when we get near Sumter and they blow us clean out of the water and straight to our Maker?"

"It don't have to go that way," Robert argued. "It's only seven miles to the blockade boats. I'll think of something."

The "something" turned out to be a broad-brimmed straw hat belonging to the *Planter*'s Confederate commander. Alfred Gridiron, the fireman-engineer, clapped it on Small's head for a joke one afternoon when the three white officers went ashore for the night. The Negro crewmen laughed.

"Look at Bob. Doggone if he ain't a ringer for ol' Cap'n Relyea. Same build, same gait. Just a little darker, is all." Smalls laughed the hardest because he suddenly saw a joke big enough to last them their lifetimes, if they lived through the making of it. He explained it to them and in the first hours of May 13, 1862, they were ready.

The *Planter* lay at Southern Wharf, her boilers cold in the engine room, her officers warm in their beds at home. Fifty yards inshore, the sentry at General Ripley's headquarters sang out "One o'clock and all is well." Robert smiled in grim agreement as he and Alfred stepped out of the captain's cabin carrying a load of pistols and rifles.

They distributed the weapons to the other six men. Then they waited.

At three in the morning Smalls said to Alfred, "Get up steam." At three-thirty, he took the wheel. The *Planter* chugged upstream and anchored near Atlantic Wharf. Aboard the steamer *Etowah,* Negro seamen had kept five womenfolk and three children of the *Planter*'s crew in hiding since nightfall. Hannah, Elizabeth and little Robert were among them. All were transferred to the *Planter* by rowboat. Then the steamer headed into the open waters of the bay. Approaching the danger point, Smalls turned the wheel over to Sam Chisholm. Then he slipped into Relyea's gold-braided coat, pulled the floppy straw hat down on his head and leaned on the windowsill of the pilothouse with arms folded. A few minutes later, holding his pose, he was staring into the muzzles of Sumter's deadly artillery.

Now!

Lazily, Smalls reached up for the cord of the steam whistle and signaled—three long, one short. An endless moment later, the order: "Pa-a-a-a-ss the *Pla-a-an-tu-u--uh!*" So far, so good. Beyond the range of the harbor guns, Smalls signaled the engine room for full speed ahead, straight for the Union fleet. The lookouts on Sumter saw, and gave the alarm, too late.

Jebel Turner hauled down the Confederate ensign and raised the white flag of truce, a bedsheet, while Smalls steered for the U.S.S. *Onward.* Aboard the blockader drums called the crew to their battle stations. A row of cannon pointed at the stolen steamer. At last, Lieutenant Nickels, aboard the *Onward,* shouted, "What vessel are you? And state your business!"

"The *Planter* out of Charleston," Smalls megaphoned, "come to join the Union fleet."[3]

[3] Philip Sterling and Rayford Logan, *Four Took Freedom,* pp. 77–78, 80–81.

This is indeed an example of courage, but it is an equally good example of intelligent problem-solving. Smalls' courage alone was not enough, but when combined with careful and critical thinking, it made him a powerful man indeed.

We need not worship the past at the expense of the present. In every age there are men who face and solve difficult problems. Leonard Kenworthy and Erma Ferrari, in *Leaders of New Nations,* give us verbal portraits of sixteen leaders who led newly independent nations after World War II. Each of these leaders faced a multitude of problems, problems which threatened the existence of his nation as a nation. As an example, the following excerpt gives a good indication of the problems faced by David Ben-Gurion and the people of the infant state of Israel:

But Ben-Gurion and his fellow Israelis could not devote all their time to external relations, important as they were and are. They had to build a nation, reclaim and develop a desert land, mold a culture, form a government, and solve many other problems.

Ben-Gurion was elected Prime Minister of the new nation of Israel. His was a gigantic undertaking. There had been nothing like it before in history. As Ben-Gurion pointed out, "Unlike other nations, we have not centuries at our disposal. Israel must accomplish in a few years what has taken others generations."

The most obvious task before them was to aid the thousands of immigrants who were pouring into Israel. Altogether there were well over a million more people in Israel at the end of its first ten years than there had been at the outset. There were 900,000 immigrants, and 300,000 more by natural increase.

These people were from seventy-nine countries of the

world. They were all Jews, but they had little in common. Many of them did not even speak Yiddish, the everyday language of many Jews. Very few of them knew Hebrew, the official language of their new homeland.

Furthermore, they had learned over the centuries the ways of life of the countries from which they came, and wanted different kinds of food, different kinds of clothing, and different kinds of shelter.

Most of those who came had lived in cities and preferred to live in large centers of population in Israel. But what Israel needed was fewer city dwellers and more farmers.

Some of them came with high enthusiasm for the new land, but many of them were tired, beaten, depressed by years of isolation and persecution or by recent troubles in their former homelands.

The immigrants from Western or Central Europe came with a good education, but most of those from Asia, the Middle East, North Africa, and Eastern Europe had little or no formal education.

In health, too, many of them were deficient. They needed medical care and good food before they could be of much use to this struggling state.

The problems which confronted Israel, however, were not all concerned with these new settlers. Israel needed to survey its new territory and to discover its resources—the minerals and the land that could be irrigated or developed in other ways to make it productive. It needed roads and ports and hundreds of miles of pipelines to carry water to irrigate the desert.

Then, too, Israel was torn asunder by the differences among religious factions and political parties. Among the extremists were a few who did not even recognize the new government, for they believed that Israel should be a religious community rather than a political state. Then there was a large group who frowned upon modern practices like mixed swimming and dancing and looked upon Ben-Gurion and other leaders as far too liberal.

These and other differences led to the organization of twenty-one different political parties that entered candidates in the first general elections in 1949.

Added to all this was the problem of finance. The new settlers brought little if any money with them and could not start earning anything for at least a few weeks or months. And the government was desperately in need of capital for all the developments it felt were necessary.

With such unsettled conditions and changes in ways of living, there were bound to be people who felt insecure and who took out their frustrations on others. So, like other nations, Israel was confronted with the problems of juvenile delinquency and adult dislocation.

In the face of such obstacles, it would take strong men and women and young people to launch a new nation. It would also take plenty of idealism, good organization, top-notch leadership, sacrifice, and adjustment.[4]

How Ben-Gurion and the Israeli people attacked some of these problems is also discussed here. This book, and others like it, can help learners realize that Israel and some of the other new nations bear living witness to man's ability to solve problems of staggering magnitude. Other instances in our history attest to the devastating consequences of failing to approach problems critically and intelligently.

We sometimes use other terms when we want to talk about a particular kind of problem-solving. One example of this is the case of military strategy. Military strategy is a particular kind of problem-solving in which major elements are the prediction of how one's opponent will react to any "move" made and the attempt to make a move which has not been pre-

[4] Leonard Kenworthy and Erma Ferrari, *Leaders of New Nations*, pp. 193–95.

dicted by the opponent. This does *not* mean that *war* is a kind of thoughtful problem-solving, but only that some aspects of a war—military strategy—do involve critical thinking. For learners interested in military history, many books are available which make clear the problem-solving tasks of the commanders. One such book is Leon Phillips' *The Fantastic Breed: Americans in King George's War*. This book chronicles the capture from the French of the fortress at Louisbourg on Cape Breton Island in 1745. Throughout the book there are discussions of the decisions made by the commanders of both the British and Colonial forces and by the French commander at Louisbourg. The following excerpt gives some indication of the difficulties involved in making the initial decision to attack the fortress:

A commission composed of some of Great Britain's highest-ranking generals and admirals made a study of Louisbourg's defenses shortly after the outbreak of the Seven Years' War, based on their admittedly incomplete military information. Even the fragments at hand convinced them that an attack on the fort no matter how strong or how heavily supported, would inevitably fail.

Commodore Sir Peter Warren was not only familiar with the recommendation, but actually had read its conclusions to the colonial officers gathered in Boston. Less than two weeks had passed since this sobering information had been passed along, and none of the officers had forgotten any of the grim details.

It was small wonder, then, that those who were attending the secret meetings were convinced that Codfish King Vaughan had lost his senses.

If the royal commission had rejected the idea of British Regulars, escorted by a powerful fleet, attacking Louisbourg, how could colonial amateurs take the fortress? The majority of militiamen had never fired a musket or rifle in battle, and the only ships available for escort purposes would be Warren's own small squadron. The attempt, the Commodore said, would be disastrous.

William Vaughan refused to back down. He was aware of the hazards, he said cheerfully, but felt certain they could be overcome. Wasn't it true, he asked Warren, that the French fleet was busy in European waters, trying to maintain a defense against the larger, more powerful British navy?

Warren had to admit that, in all probability, there were few French warships stationed at Louisbourg.

Vaughan then turned to General Pepperrell. Wasn't it true, he demanded, that Louisbourg was the very last place the French expected an attack?

The commander-in-chief of the American forces had to concede that the French wouldn't dream of such an assault.

Wasn't it also true, the mettlesome Maine District officer wanted to know, that surprise attacks on forts usually enjoyed the greatest success?

Again Pepperrell reluctantly agreed.

By now, others were becoming interested in the idea. It was so daring that many of the officers were intrigued, in spite of themselves, and even Pepperrell and Warren, the two men whose word would be final, had fallen thoughtfully silent.

At the worst, Colonel Vaughan continued, an expedition would be driven off. If it appeared that losses would be heavy, the British-American flotilla could retreat. He was so convinced the chances of victory were good, however, that he offered the use of the largest and sturdiest fishing vessels in his fleet as troop transports.

By now the members of the war council were taking the proposal seriously. If Vaughan was willing to risk the loss of expensive fishing schooners that could not be replaced in wartime, it was apparent that he had weighed the odds and found them favorable.

Governor Shirley, unlike the military men, had not yet recovered from his initial astonishment. Was there really a possibility, he asked, that Louisbourg could be captured?

Pepperrell replied in a brief address that was transcribed by his aides. When published several years later, it won him lasting renown in military circles. "Any defenses erected by man can be destroyed by man," he said. "Intelligent planning, careful execution of that plan, consistent demonstrations of courage by the offensive corps, and sound leadership can achieve any goal, provided the initial considerations are realistic. It would be absurd for one hundred men to attack a strong fort defended by one thousand, but those same one hundred might have a far better chance if the fort were held by a like number."[5]

From reading such accounts, learners may see not only the importance of critical thinking, but also the difficulty of making important decisions on the basis of very sketchy evidence and information.

An historical work which places more emphasis on failure than success in facing problems is Lloyd Robinson's *The Hopefuls: Ten Presidential Campaigns*. In this book we look at presidential campaigns from the point of view of the unsuccessful candidates. What accounts for a loss in a political campaign? Clearly there are many factors which must be considered. One important consideration, although surely not the only one, is the political strategy. Political strategy, like military strategy, is a kind of problem-solving. A now classic case of faulty strategy in a presidential campaign is that of Thomas E. Dewey in the 1948 election.

[5] Leon Phillips, *The Fantastic Breed*, pp. 46–48.

As the election campaign began in September, the public-opinion polls gave their verdict on Truman's chances: zero. The Roper survey found Dewey ahead 44 percent to 31 percent, and commented, "All the evidence we have accumulated since 1936 tends to indicate that the man in the lead at the beginning of the campaign is the man who is the winner at the end of it." Roper's conclusion was that Dewey was so far ahead "that we might just as well get ready to listen to his inauguration on January 20, 1949."

Truman refused to give up hope. He launched a campaign that would take him 31,000 miles through the country by train to address some six million people. The President slashed at those old Democratic foes, Wall Street and the millionaires of industry. "They are not satisfied with being rich," he said. "They want to increase their power and their privileges, regardless of what happens to the other fellow. They are gluttons of privilege."

Repeatedly Truman spoke of the "do-nothing" Congress, calling it "a sample of what a Republican administration would mean to you." He told the farmers of the Midwest how the Republicans had "stuck a pitchfork" in their backs by turning down his farm-aid programs. He reminded his listeners of the "Harding-Coolidge boom and the Hoover Depression."

While the President was delivering his blistering speeches, Governor Dewey was taking a calmer approach. On September 20, in his first major campaign address, he ignored all of Truman's charges and spoke as though the election were already won: "Tonight we will enter upon a campaign to unite America. On January 20 we will enter upon a new era. We propose to install in Washington an administration which has faith in the American people, a warm understanding of their needs, and the confidence to meet them."

His tone remained calm and cool while Truman grew more fiery. In Arizona, Dewey declared, "Ours is a magnificent land. . . . Don't let anybody frighten you or try to stampede you into believing that America is finished." Progress, though, had to come from private enterprise, not the government, he said. "If it had been up to Washington to develop, let us say, our electrical industry, you can be pretty sure we'd still be using kerosene lamps." Dewey spoke in vague, relaxing terms, telling the voters to have "faith in America" and be of "stout purpose and a full heart" and "move forward shoulder to shoulder." As the sure winner, Dewey did not intend to spoil his chances by getting down into an ugly brawl of charges and counter-charges.

Truman's salty approach drew big crowds as he journeyed across the country. Laughing, cheering Americans applauded him even when he blew his lines, threw wild punches at Dewey, or lost track of his own arguments. It only made him seem more human, while Dewey, as one political commentator put it, was "a machine with a cellophane cover."

Sensing his opportunity, Truman closed in on Dewey's very smoothness: "The leopard has not changed his spots; he has merely hired some public-relations experts. And they have taught him to wear sheep's clothing and to purr sweet nothings about unity in a soothing voice. But it's the same old leopard." A few days later, Truman poked fun at Dewey's "efficiency," saying, "We remember that there never was such a gang of efficiency engineers in Washington as there was under Herbert Hoover. We remember Mr. Hoover was himself a great efficiency expert."

Unruffled, Dewey pointed out to the nation how badly the President had handled some delicate negotiations with Russia over the status of Berlin, and how inefficient he had been in halting crippling strikes. "We all know the sad record of the present administration. More than three years have passed since the end of the war and it has failed to win the peace. Millions upon millions of people have been delivered into Soviet slavery, while our own administration has tried appeasement on one day and bluster the next. Our country desperately needs new and better leadership in the cause of peace and freedom."

It was easy for Dewey to show Harry Truman's flaws as President. Truman had plenty of human failings, as he was the first to admit. When it came to suggesting programs of his own, though, Dewey said little. That allowed Truman to comment that the whole Republican campaign could be summed up in two phrases: "Me too" and "We're against it."

Dewey brushed aside Truman's stinging words. As November arrived, he was thinking about the men he would name to his cabinet, and perhaps was already planning the inaugural address of President Dewey. *Life* ran Dewey's picture with the caption, "The next President of the United States." The New York *Times* predicted that Dewey would win with 345 electoral votes. Truman, the *Times* said, would carry only eleven states. The Gallup poll, the day before the election, gave Dewey 49.5 percent of the vote, Truman 44.5 percent, Wallace 4 percent, Thurmond 2 percent. Elmo Roper's final figures were even more emphatic: Dewey 52.2 percent, Truman 37.1 percent, Thurmond 5.2 percent, Wallace 4.3 percent, and the Socialist candidate Norman Thomas 0.6 percent. "I stand by my prediction," Roper said. "Mr. Dewey is in."

All that remained was the counting of the ballots. That would make the Dewey victory official.

On the night of November 2, a puzzling trend showed up in the early returns. Truman seemed to be ahead. The Republicans were not worried, though. These returns came from eastern cities, always Democratic strongholds. Soon votes would be arriving from the centers of Republican power—the small towns, the farms, the suburban districts. "This is definitely a Republican year," Dewey's campaign manager said. Truman's early lead would vanish by ten o'clock, and by midnight Dewey would be a clear winner.

The newspapers agreed. DEWEY DEFEATS TRUMAN, screamed the headline of the early edition of the Chicago *Tribune*. The New York *Daily Mirror*'s early edition declared: "First returns . . . indicated that Governor Thomas E. Dewey and the Republican ticket were headed for a popular vote margin and a possible electoral-vote landslide." And the counting of votes went on. Dewey fell further and further behind. Truman, who had gone to sleep early, was awakened by friends just after midnight and shown the surprising figures.

When dawn came, the Truman lead remained—though in some states he was ahead by just a few thousand votes. Dewey told reporters that he was "still confident." The morning newspapers came out, containing political columns written well in advance that speculated about the make-up of President Dewey's cabinet, and the Democrats read them with vast amusement.

The end came at 11:14 A.M. California and Ohio had definitely gone Democratic, the vote-counters announced. Truman had won the election! A broadly grinning President appeared, holding on high the Chicago newspaper with its huge DEWEY DEFEATS TRUMAN headline. Dewey, stunned and baffled, had achieved the impossible, turning certain victory into incredible defeat. He was the most amazed man in the country that Wednesday morning—except perhaps for the poll-takers.[6]

What are learners to find out about problem-solving from this example? We know that all sorts of politicians have read all sorts of meaning into this election, and we will not try to do that here. But without being too unfair to Dewey, we might suggest that learners consider whether he did not fail in the initial task facing any problem-solver: recognizing the problem.

Another book by Robinson deals with a presidential

[6] Lloyd Robinson, *The Hopefuls*, pp. 108–12.

candidate who succeeded in getting a majority of the
popular vote but failed to be elected by the Electoral
College. This, of course, was Samuel Tilden. The title
of the book is *The Stolen Election: Hayes Versus
Tilden 1876*. Robinson discusses not only the facts
surrounding the disputed election but also the consequences of "resolving" the dispute as it was resolved:

And so it was finished. The men of 1876 were gone;
the scandal faded into history, and most Americans forgot
that there was a time when one man had won the presi-
dency and another had taken the White House.

What were the effects of that event? How was history
changed? Did it matter, really, whether Hayes or Tilden
had been sworn in?

It mattered. Hayes was the President of reconciliation.
He buried the bloody shirt, forgave the South for its rebel-
lion and drew the nation together after the decades of bitterness. As a Republican, as a Civil War veteran who had
been wounded to save the Union, Hayes could do this.
Tilden could not. As a Democrat, as a man with no war
record, he would not have been in a strong enough position.
Whatever he did to help the South would have been regarded in the North as treason. Hayes was bitterly enough
blamed for his kindly treatment of the South, but at least
he could not be accused of secret Confederate leanings.
He saved the nation from the danger of continued strife
between North and South.

Tilden saved the nation too, great patriot that he was.
If he had tried to claim by force what the people wished
him to have, war might have resulted. Only a man of tow-
ering character could have turned his back on the presi-
dency so that no bloodshed would be caused. He stood
aside voluntarily. That was the measure of his greatness.

The nation gained because Hayes put an end to the evils

of Radical Reconstruction. Whether he did it freely or because he had made a political deal is beside the point; he cast the carpetbaggers down, and made the Southerners their own masters again. In other ways, though, the 1876 election worked great harm.

Most obvious is the harm done to democracy. The vote of the people was ignored. This was something that should never have happened, and must never happen again.

The country was deprived of the services of Samuel J. Tilden—a great reformer, a great administrator. Whether Tilden would have been able to function effectively as President in the tense United States of 1877–80 we can never know; but he should have had the chance.

The crime of 1876 had a powerful effect on future generations, too. It robbed the American Negro of his voice in political life, and brought about injustices that are only now being corrected. In a way, it called back and canceled the accomplishments of the Civil War.

Men had fought and died to free the slaves. After the war, the Republicans had emerged as the champions of the Negro. They went too far, though, committing the excesses of Reconstruction, forcing the defeated southern whites to submit to the rule of their own ex-slaves. Placing illiterate Negroes into positions of power created hatred among the whites that still has not died away. But the storms of Reconstruction eventually brought about something even worse: the recapture by the whites of a dominant position, and the loss of all civil rights by the Negroes.

This would have happened eventually even if Tilden had won, since all but three southern states had been redeemed by 1876. But the events of that year finished the job. The troops were taken out of the South; the white Democrats were given control; and the Republicans, in their eagerness to have the White House, abandoned the Negroes to their fate. The deal between Hayes and the South left the whites free to do as they pleased with their black neighbors, confident that there would be no Federal interference. As the liberal *Nation* said sadly, "The Negro will disappear from the field of national politics. Henceforth the nation, as a nation, will have nothing more to do with him." And the New York *Tribune* said farewell to the era of Negro power in the South with a typical example of the thinking of the times. The Negroes, said the *Tribune,* "after ample opportunity to develop their own latent capacities," had merely proven that "as a race they are idle, ignorant, and vicious."

Governor Wade Hampton of South Carolina did his best to work for Negro rights, as he had promised when President Hayes put him in office. He gave the Negroes better schools, honest justice, protection from white racists and a number of state jobs. As his reward, he was overthrown and defeated by the white people of his state.

Night descended once more for the Negro of the South. He lost the right to vote, to hold office, to exercise the ordinary privileges of any citizen. The restored white rulers were determined to make up for the years when Negroes had enjoyed the favor of the carpetbaggers. The southern states prohibited Negroes from going to the same schools as whites, from entering churches or theaters used by whites, from eating at the same restaurants. The Negro was no longer a slave, but otherwise he was reduced to second-class citizenship. Negroes who protested were beaten or killed. And the Republican Party, once the great defender of the Negro, did nothing. This was the worst heritage of the Compromise of 1877. It broke the alliance between Republicans and Negroes that had come out of the Civil War, and condemned black Americans to eighty more years of misery before the national government once again began to fight for the rights of these oppressed people.

There had never been an election like that of 1876 in American history before. There has never been one since, although the electoral system has not greatly changed, and an extremely close election might well have the same chaotic outcome. The Hayes-Tilden contest produced a sorry spectacle. The forces that controlled it are still with us: the bitterness between white man and black, the hunger for power, the willingness to betray high ideals when high office is at stake. Probably we will be spared the turmoil and the agony of a disputed electoral count again, but the possibility remains alive.[7]

It may be of no use to debate what *might* have happened had different decisions been made. However, learners should see that consequences of decisions which have been made are matters of fact, and as such are relevant information to be taken into account in future decisions. We can learn from bad decisions as well as good ones.

Problem-solving, we have said repeatedly, is not the province of leaders alone but is something we all do, sometimes well and sometimes badly. To find out how other men have reacted to *their* problems can sometimes help us as we face our own. Biographies often serve this purpose well. Dorothy and Joseph Samachson in *Masters of Music: Their Works, Their Lives, Their Times* have provided biographical sketches of great and near-great musicians. Learners reading this book will find that many of these men faced serious obstacles, that problems in their personal lives threatened their work as artists. Some, the reader learns, overcame the problems, while others let the problems overcome them. Here, again, learners could be encouraged to learn from both the failures and the successes of other people.

There is another part of this same book which could be used by the interested teacher to get learners actively engaged in the process of critical thinking. The

[7] Lloyd Robinson, *The Stolen Election*, pp. 225–29.

following excerpt, entitled "Half the Human Race," is the concluding section of *Masters of Music:*

The reader may have noted what appears to be a rather strange omission: of the many great and near-great composers we have listed, only one has been a woman. Women have been outstanding performers, and one of the most famous teachers of contemporary composers is a Frenchwoman, Nadia Boulanger (1887–   ). She and her sister, Lili (1893–1918), were the first two women to win the *Prix de Rome,* a prize given solely for talent in composition. Nevertheless, their own music is rarely if ever played.

Many women have composed music (the name of Clara Schumann comes to mind), but what has prevented them from composing music of such beauty that their works would be part of the concert repertoire?

Was it the Catholic Church, because it did not permit them to become church musicians? There are other churches, and none of the evidence indicates that non-Catholic women have written better music than Catholic women. Was it discrimination by male musicians? There has been discrimination against women performing, but our leading symphony orchestras include women instrumentalists as well as men. Was it lack of dedication? Perhaps. But many women have shown fierce dedication to their careers in acting, singing, and writing. Why not in composing?

None of these reasons, in itself, appears to be valid. Perhaps it is a combination of all three that has prevented women from composing great music. We cannot be sure. We have said that music is many languages. Now we must add that while the female half of the human race is able to understand the languages of music spoken by others, and can express the musical thoughts of others, it has so far not uttered worthwhile thoughts of its own.[8]

[8] Dorothy and Joseph Samachson, *Masters of Music,* pp. 257–58.

How *does* one explain the fact that there have been so few women composers? This is a question which calls for hypotheses, evidence to test those hypotheses, and all of the other steps we have discussed as parts of the process of critical thinking. It is a question which invites the active participation of learners in seeking an adequate answer. And it is a problem which needs to be solved, both to explain our musical past and to make it possible to alter conditions so that our musical future can be enriched by the other "half."

Many books read by learners today tell of how man has increased his control over his environment, how he has solved some of the problems presented by his natural world. One such book is Robert Kraske's *Crystals of Life: The Story of Salt.* This book tells not only of man's dependency on salt, but also how man has used salt to solve other problems and, hence, to improve the quality of his life. The following is one example of such problem-solving:

Salt provided the key to one of man's great triumphs in public health.

In Michigan in the 1920s, medical authorities were faced with a major health problem. As many as two persons in five were disfigured with goiter, an ugly swelling of the throat. In severe cases, the goiter grew as large as an orange or grapefruit. Among 32,000 school children examined, nearly half showed symptoms of this disease. Even stray dogs had swollen throats.

U. S. Public Health Service doctors investigated the problem and soon found the answer. Goiter developed when people lacked an essential chemical in their systems: iodine. In Michigan, farm soil lacked this vital chemical. Vegetables, fruits, and grains grew without it, and thus people did not get it in their diet. Goiter resulted when the thyroid gland began swelling in reaction to the lack of iodine it needed to function normally.

Doctors had found the solution, but now they faced the question: How could you treat an entire population threatened with goiter?

Salt provided the answer they needed.

Public health officials asked salt makers to add iodine to table salt in the ratio of one pound for every ten thousand pounds of salt. Everyone ate salt, they reasoned. Thus everyone—an entire population—could be treated to prevent goiter. This is the salt that today is labeled "iodized salt."

So successful was salt as a carrier for iodine that goiter vanished as a public-health problem in Michigan.

"Even mongrel dogs roaming city streets now have normal thyroids," remarked one doctor.[9]

Learners will also find in this book a warning that in solving some of our problems we often create others. The following passage discusses a problem which, if we do not guard against it, could appear in the future.

About one hundred years ago, the people of North America were convinced that their supply of trees was inexhaustible. So, in the space of about thirty years, the great forests of Wisconsin and Michigan were obliterated. Big trees were cut down and sawed into boards and small trees were crushed by lumberjacks, machines, and by falling trees. No thought was given to conservation, and men moved on—leaving desolation behind them.

About fifty years ago, the people of this continent were convinced that their fertile soil was inexhaustible. So they used the soil, never replenishing its nutrients, never thinking of using the soil wisely. The result was that, by the

[9] Robert Kraske, *Crystals of Life: The Story of Salt*, p. 121.

middle of the 1930s, an estimated 100 million acres had been ruined in the United States alone. Another 125 million acres were in the process of being ruined, and the men moved on—leaving desolation behind them.

Just a few years ago, the people of this continent were convinced that their supply of water was unlimited. But now we are paying for our misuse of water; many parts of this country are experiencing a critical water shortage. According to one scientific estimate, the water supply in the United States is only enough to support about 230 million people, while the Census Bureau expects our population to pass that mark sometime between 1975 and 1978.

Time after time, man has thought that his natural resources were inexhaustible—only to discover that he was rapidly approaching the point of total exhaustion of these resources. Can this be true for salt, too?

It would appear that we truly have an inexhaustible supply of salt. "The reserve of salt in the United States has been estimated at 60,000 billion tons," states the U. S. Department of the Interior's Bureau of Mines—enough salt at today's rate of use to supply all the nations of the world for the next six hundred thousand years! The Bureau concludes: "Conservation [of salt] is seldom considered."

But let us take a closer look. To begin with, more people exist on earth today than ever before. And they all need salt. In 1650, only one-half billion people lived on earth. Two hundred years later, there were twice that number. But by 1920, the population had doubled again to two billion. As you can see, this time the doubling of the population took only seventy years instead of two hundred. Only forty years later, one billion more people occupied the earth. Today, our population of over three billion people has begun to crowd this planet.

At the same time that the world's population is increasing by leaps and bounds, industry is finding new uses for salt. Not only do we have more people who demand salt, we also have more uses for salt than ever before.

Add to this the fact that we are, to some small extent, polluting our present sources of salt—by storing radioactive wastes in salt mines, for example, and by dumping industrial waste into the ocean—and a tiny problem begins to appear. More people need more salt. More industries need more salt. And we have slowly begun to pollute some sources of this precious material.

Despite these small indications of waste and the increased demands on the world's salt supply, we do not think that a shortage will ever develop in the civilized world. However, it would pay us to keep some facts of history in mind. The human race seems to have a talent for destroying its natural resources rather than for using them wisely. Let us, therefore, keep in mind that while it may not *now* be necessary to conserve salt, we do not want our children or our children's children to blame us for squandering this—our most vital mineral resource.[10]

Learners should be encouraged to think about the questions which this passage raises. Is this a problem? When does a problem become a problem? Have some "solutions" to our problems in the past been worth the eventual cost? Does expediency sometimes masquerade as problem-solving?

Perhaps we can get some good clues about how to answer these questions by looking at some problems which are already with us. The natural resources about which we are most concerned today are air and water, resources that in the past were taken for granted. An excellent book for young readers dealing with the problems of air and water pollution is Dorothy E. Shuttlesworth's, *Clean Air—Sparkling Water: The Fight Against Pollution*. The following, an excerpt from Part I, "A Fable of Two Communities," is a

[10] Robert Kraske, *op. cit.* pp. 137–39.

rather lengthy but excellent example of how a community might begin to solve the problem of air pollution:

In the town everyone was calling for help: the mayor, the department of health, the people themselves. Everyone wondered what was happening.

Experts explained about the temperature inversion and the dirt. But little could be done to clear the air. The best advice they could give people was to stay indoors.

Fortunately, on the fourth day after the temperature inversion began, there was a change in temperatures and winds started to blow. Slowly the dark, heavy fog began to lift, and after a while the air was clear. It almost seemed that the three black days had been a bad dream.

But it was no dream. People had died. Pets had died. Everywhere gardens had wilted. The killer fog had been very real. Another like it could come at any time. Where could help be found?

The people soon discovered there was no one to turn to. A town meeting was called. The mayor asked who would serve on a committee to investigate the danger that threatened them. Everyone was anxious to help, and soon a committee of ten citizens was chosen. It was called simply the Clean Air Committee, or the CAC.

At first the CAC blamed the city across the river for the dirty air. They saw the smoke pouring out from the city's factories all day and sometimes during the night.

Close to the riverfront of the city there was other smoke coming from dumping grounds where refuse was burned. Still more rose from apartment houses that burned garbage in incinerators. And great amounts poured out from electric-power plants.

The activities of the big city were a large part of the reason that the air in the town was polluted, for often the poisons blew across the river. But one discovery made by the people of the town surprised and shocked them. Not all of their troubles from pollution were coming from across the river. Some pollution was being created right in and around their own homes.

Not only the Clean Air Committee was studying the deadly conditions. Boys and girls in the school science classes became detectives, looking for clues that would tell how the air was being made unhealthy and destroying the beauty of their town.

One thing they investigated was how air currents behave. To do so, they took turns inflating balloons. Then, before releasing the balloons from a rooftop, they fastened a note to each string-tie, stating the place, date, and time the balloon was set free. The note also asked that anyone finding the balloon get in touch with the school—for the sake of air-pollution studies. Soon calls were being received. Some were from miles away. It was easy to understand how winds that carried balloons could also carry fumes and bits of dirt.

Other studies were made with instruments such as the wet- and dry-bulb thermometer, which could measure the relative humidity in the air. A knowledge of the state of the atmosphere was helpful in knowing when to expect especially bad pollution problems.

The people learned that not just a few sources of air pollution exist, but hundreds of thousands. Of course, only one of them might be enough to poison one particular area. They learned that some pollution sources can easily be eliminated while others, it seems, are impossible to correct. But improvements in controlling them can always be made.

One discovery was that the burning of leaves contributed to air pollution. Some people burned trash regularly in their own back-yard incinerators. And this burning sent ash and fumes into the air. Worst of all was a city dump where large pieces of junk—including old cars—were burned.

Some of the older homes had coal-burning furnaces.

From their chimneys came fly ash—the part of coal that does not burn. It played a part in polluting the air.

And of course the investigators considered the pollution problem caused by the exhaust from motor vehicles. Private cars, buses—all contributed. If the people of the town could find a way to correct the troubles caused by such vehicles, they would be solving one of the greatest pollution problems in the entire nation!

Naturally, the more cars that are crowded together, the worse is the effect of their exhaust fumes. So the town was not suffering from this kind of pollution as much as a large city did.

However, the Clean Air Committee urged that everyone keep his car in good condition so that the least possible amount of pollution would be created. It was often hard work to persuade people that everyone must take part in bringing back clean air. Even if this meant spending money to tune up old cars. Even if it meant finding other ways to get rid of trash than burning it in the open. Even if it meant giving up bonfires.[11]

Learners will be able to recognize in the above passage many of the steps in the problem-solving process. They will probably recognize as well some familiar difficulties. The CAC's initial response of placing all the blame on the city across the river, for example, strikes a familiar chord. When we are faced with a problem, it is tempting to say that someone else caused it, or at least that someone else should solve it. Learners should also be helped to see that a large part of the task was that of clarifying the problem. Air pollution cannot be stopped until its causes are determined. It always sounds easy when someone says

[11] Dorothy Shuttlesworth, *Clean Air—Sparkling Water,* pp. 21–28.

that the first step is recognizing and clarifying the problem, but this is often a complex and difficult task indeed. And let us not overlook the fact that the problem of pollution is a problem created by man's shortsighted "solutions" to other problems.

It is not only shortsighted solutions which create new problems. As we have said before, we need to view problem-solving as a continuing kind of behavior rather than as something which, once performed, removes the need for further thought. Many books reinforce this point. The following passage in Irmengarde Eberle's *Koalas Live Here* is a case in point:

There had been a time, not so very many years ago, when men hunted koalas for their fur. At last there were only a few left in all eastern Australia, where there once had been many thousands. Then the Australian Government had made laws protecting these animals. Since then, generations after generations of young koalas have been allowed to grow up and have young ones. And so the few who had survived the shootings of the hunters began to grow into little colonies, and then into larger ones.

Because of this protection from the Government, our koala family of three was alive and browsing in the forest today.

But now, though there was no longer danger from hunters with guns, the many koalas in this particular place were facing another serious trouble. It was trouble that could kill them as surely as bullets. The problem was that this whole region with its burned-out forest, and the overeaten branches of the surviving trees, could no longer give these animals enough of their necessary food. They were in danger of starving.

Our koala family ate what they could find, but they were almost always hungry now.[12]

[12] Irmengarde Eberle, *Koalas Live Here,* pp. 40, 43.

This is an excellent example of how a solution to one problem, even though it is a *good* solution, may create another problem. Critical thinking, as learners will see, is not likely to become obsolete. As we solve a problem we set the stage for a new problem to appear.

It is important for learners to understand that not all problems are easily solved and not all questions are quickly answered, even when those questions and problems have to do with phenomena we observe daily. In *The Miracle of Flight* by Richard Cromer there is a discussion of what man has learned about birds' ability to fly. There is also a description of the continuing but not yet successful attempts to solve the problem of the way migrating birds navigate:

So far, other experiments, including radar observations, seem to confirm the ability of birds to navigate by the stars. Bouncing radio signals from the dark sky detects flocks of smaller birds and even some of the individual larger birds. These radar observations show that birds fly confidently on *starry* nights, but become confused about direction on *cloudy* nights when the stars aren't visible.

The full story of migration obviously cannot be told, for no one knows it yet. The more we learn about it, the more remarkable the real explanation will need to be. Meanwhile, the collection of theories grows, and if we haven't the right answer yet, it isn't because we lack imagination.

Other Explanations

Many proposed explanations involve special senses the birds might have. We know dogs and other animals have highly developed senses of smell that they use in direction-finding. Perhaps birds have some additional sense beyond those five that we know about: hearing, sight, touch, taste, and smell. One theory suggests birds might be able to sense infrared heat waves, and that they find their way from place to place by reading these radiations from the earth.

A still more complicated theory suggests that birds are able to detect the earth's magnetic field and use this to find their way. But to navigate with a magnetic compass, the bird must be able to adjust it to the constantly varying strength of the earth's field. In addition, these magnetic lines of force run in just one general direction—north and south. The bird would need still another device for determining its east-west position.

Nevertheless, experiments have been conducted to see if there is anything to this magnetic-field theory. Small, permanent magnets have been attached to homing-pigeons' heads, to the tips of their wings, and hung from strings around their necks. The idea was that if birds really could sense the earth's magnetic field, a strong magnet near them would jam their sensing mechanisms. But the magnets had no effect on their ability to return home. And so the search goes on and on.[13]

Thus, we have a phenomenon which has been recognized over the centuries but for which we cannot yet give an adequate explanation. From reading about attempts to solve this puzzle, learners will see that we have learned, and that although we are not able to account fully for birds' ability to navigate, we have gathered enough information to know that some suggested explanations will not do.

Another book which describes some of man's attempts to improve his understanding of the natural world is Roy A. Gallant and Christopher J. Schuberth's, *Discovering Rocks and Minerals*. Among the

[13] Richard Cromer, *The Miracle of Flight*, p. 149.

things the reader will encounter in this work is an excellent account of how paleontologists have used fossil evidence to piece together a partial history of our planet:

All of our knowledge of past life is based on fossils and the rocks in which they are found. Fossils tell us that all present-day plants and animals have primitive ancestors that lived on the earth many millions of years ago. In most cases, the very old ancestral plants and animals were not able to go on living and reproducing themselves; they died out, or became extinct. All we know about the dinosaurs and other extinct organisms comes from a study of their fossil remains.

Fossils also tell us something about the position of seas and land masses of the past. Such animals as corals, brachiopods, and trilobites have lived only in the sea. By following the curving shoreline of an ancient inland sea now marked by rock containing marine fossils, we can trace the outline of that sea. Two thousand years ago the Greeks clearly saw in the fossil remains signs that land areas had sunk and risen at various times. (But others believed the fossils to be only the remains of some "ancient worker's lunch.") The trunks of fossil trees found where they originally grew tell us of a former land area. We then know that an ancient sea did not cover that area at the time the trees were growing.

Paleontologists can also find out about the climate of the past by studying fossils. What would you think if you found fossil tree ferns or fossil magnolias in Antarctica or Greenland? Such plants were actually found in those places. You would have to say that the climate there was indeed much warmer at that time, perhaps a tropical climate. Coal deposits often contain tree ferns and other plants. These plants suggest, again, a rather warm and swampy region during the time the coal deposits were forming. But today many of these coal deposits are found in parts of the world that are quite cold and dry. The climate had to be much different then from what it is today in those places in order for warm swamplands to have existed.

But we still have not talked about one of the most important uses of fossils. Fossils give us very important clues about the age of the rocks that contain them. Let us see how this was first discovered.

During the seventeenth century, scientists knew for certain that the older rock strata are covered by younger ones. The arrangement of these layers in such an orderly sequence is known as the law of superposition. This law states that, in a normal sequence of strata, younger rocks are always found on top of older ones.

Around the year 1800, an English surveyor and civil engineer named William Smith learned that the success of different engineering projects—particularly the building of canals—depended on the kind of rock strata found in the region where the canal was to be dug. As he studied different rock layers, he saw that many of them had fossils. Soon he noticed that any single rock layer usually contained the same assemblage of fossils. The younger rock layers above, and the older rock layers below, each had different kinds of fossils. Soon, Smith became so skillful that whenever he saw a fossil he could tell from which layer of rock the fossil was collected.

At about the same time, two French geologists were studying and mapping the extent of the fossil-bearing strata that surround Paris. Both Georges Cuvier and Alexandre Brongniart also discovered that certain fossils were found only in certain rock layers. These two geologists also had used the law of superposition to arrange the rocks in the Paris area in chronological order, just as Smith had done in England. They, too, came to realize that each individual rock layer contained its own distinctive assemblage of fossils.

As Cuvier and Brongniart arranged their collections of fossils in the same order as the rocks from which they came, they discovered something else. They learned that the fossils changed in an orderly way from layer to layer. Cuvier and Brongniart compared the fossil forms with the more modern forms of life. It soon became evident that the fossils from the higher, and, therefore, younger, rock layers were more similar to modern forms of life than those fossils from rock strata lower down.

By studying the fossil assemblage in any layer of sedimentary rock, scientists are able to tell the *relative* age of that rock layer. This fact has been proven time and again by other geologists and paleontologists throughout the world. Each rock layer usually contains its own distinctive fossil assemblage. But the rock layers above, and those below, contain different assemblages of fossils. Over the years following the work of Smith, Cuvier, and Brongniart, more and more information about the positions of fossils in the rock layers rapidly accumulated from all parts of the world. Today it is possible to place even a single kind of fossil from any part of the world into its proper time period.

When scientists discovered that fossils could help tell them the relative age of the rock that contained them, they were then able to start to unravel the complex history of our planet.

Fossils, then, tell us two important things: (1) that certain kinds of plants and animals were living together during certain time periods when certain sediments were forming; and (2) whether the sediments were formed on a shallow sea floor, in a desert, in a river bed, or in a swamp. By carefully studying fossils and the sedimentary rock that contains them, a paleontologist can learn a lot about the past. He can, bit by bit, build up the setting for a giant and extinct reptile such as *Brontosaurus*. He can tell what this dinosaur looked like, what animal neighbors it had, the plants that it ate, and he can picture the kinds of swamps in which it lived. Like a detective, the paleontologist puts together all of the clues he can find, and from them he recalls fascinating scenes of ancient worlds.[14]

The paleontologist is indeed like a detective. What this means is that he is engaged in problem-solving and that his inferences are drawn on the basis of incomplete and indirect evidence. From this example learners can see that paleontology, like much other problem-solving, has required more for its development than a sudden stroke of genius. The success of paleontology has required as well careful and repeated attempts to explain by generating hypotheses and by testing these hypotheses with evidence obtained from careful observation.

Sometimes we are so accustomed to having an adequate solution to a problem that we do not recognize the difficulties presented by the problem in the past. One such problem is that of keeping time. John Gabriel Navarra's book *Clocks, Calendars, and Carrousels* is an account of man's attempts through history to solve the problem of keeping time. The reader finds in this work that a satisfactory method of keeping time at one point in history may be completely unsatisfactory at another: New conditions call for new ways to keep time. The following passage gives one example of how an accepted method of keeping time became obsolete:

The first railroad in America was constructed in 1826. It was built to carry granite from a quarry at Quincy,

[14] Roy A. Gallant and Christopher Schuberth, *Discovering Rocks and Minerals*, pp. 98–101.

Massachusetts, to the nearest water transportation. Only three miles of track were laid to get the job done.

The first American-made locomotives were built for the South Carolina Canal and Rail Road Company. They were in use at the end of 1830 around Charleston, South Carolina. For the next thirty years, there was a great development in rail transportation. Then in the 1860s the United States gave the Central Pacific and the Union Pacific the right to connect the eastern and the western parts of the country by rail.

The rapid building of railroads in the 1860s brought the problem of time to everyone. There were more than 300 local times used in the United States during this period. Each town had its own local sun time!

A railroad needs to run on schedule so that people know when it will arrive and when it will depart. It was impossible to make a schedule for each local sun time. From 1860 to 1883 the railroads solved this problem by setting their own time. Everyone called it "railroad time" and you had to use it to know when the trains arrived and departed.

The trains in a region all ran on one time schedule. In the east, the Pennsylvania Railroad used Philadelphia time. This meant the Pennsylvania Railroad trains set their clocks to Philadelphia sun time. Philadelphia sun time was five minutes slower than New York sun time, and it was five minutes faster than Baltimore sun time. People meeting trains had to keep this in mind if they wanted to be "on time" for a trip.

England was one of the first countries to face the problem of each town keeping its own sun time. Sir John Herschel, the famous English astronomer, asked the English to forget the sun time in local towns. He said they should fix one time for all of England. Sir John made his plans in 1828.

Of course, England is not as large as the United States. Sir John Herschel's idea made sense for a small country.

By 1850, the English put his plan to use! They used the sun time of Greenwich for all of England, Scotland, and Wales. Greenwich time became known as the *Standard Time*.

Now, you could travel anywhere in England, Scotland, or Wales and find all watches set to Greenwich sun time. But this meant that English watches were often out of step with the sun. The watches were exact only when the Englishman found himself in Greenwich. But at least everyone *spoke the same time* as well as the same language.

England is a small country. The watches were not that much out of step when Greenwich sun time was used. But the United States is a large country. The problem was much more difficult.

The sun time of one location could not be taken and used across the United States. The distance from east to west across our country is almost 3000 miles. The sun time of one location—even for a city in the middle of the country—would be too far out of step with the sun time of another section.

Special planning was needed to make standard time work in the United States. The railroads began talking about standard time in 1872. And finally, by 1883, a plan of standard *time zones* was set up.[15]

Again we have an illustration of the fact that our "tools," or conventions—our solutions to problems— which are satisfactory at one point in time become problems to be solved at a later time. Imagine the problems we would encounter today if each community kept its own local sun time!

Throughout this book references have been made to the importance of language, logic, and mathematics in critical thinking. Although a great deal of attention is

[15] John G. Navarra, *Clocks, Calendars, and Carrousels*, pp. 51–53.

paid to these concerns in the classroom, they are not common topics for treatment in most books children read outside of their regular school work. However, there are exceptions: books which learners will read and enjoy and which *do* deal with these concerns in an interesting fashion. One such book is *Probability: The Science of Chance* by Arthur G. Razzell and K. G. O. Watts. For the learner in the intermediate grades who is interested in logic and mathematics, this is an exciting book. The authors present many problems for the learner to solve, and the explanations of probability are clear and engaging. The topic of probability is introduced as follows:

Have you ever wondered what is going to happen tomorrow, or what you will do when you grow up? People have always been interested in the future and have tried in many ways to foretell what is going to happen. Telling fortunes by tea leaves left in teacups was one way; other people tried to look into the future by using playing cards, tarot cards or by studying the palm of a person's hand.

Even today there are men and women who make their living by trying to tell people what the future holds for them. Many newspapers and magazines print articles every day which try to foretell the reader's future by the stars and planets.

This book is not about fortunetellers or astrologers; it will tell you a few of the ways in which men have used mathematics and their powers of observation to predict events that are probable or likely to happen.

Although you may not be aware of it, nearly every day you make predictions about the future in very much the same way as a modern scientist or mathematician does. For example, if a friend of yours said, "Let's have a picnic this afternoon," you might say, "That's a good idea but it is cloudy and the air feels damp. It feels like rain."

By observation you have predicted the future, not *certainly*, because we all know a cloudy sky doesn't *necessarily* mean rain, but from your observations it seems as though it will *probably* rain. And that would most likely be enough for you to plan your picnic for another day.[16]

This little book does not just tell *about* problems of probability, but also provides problems for learners to solve, problems which are both important and interesting.

The importance of learning to master our language in order to think more clearly is emphasized in a sensitive and humorous way by Mary O'Neill in *Words, Words, Words*. One example is her poem "Man, Animals and Written Words":

MAN, ANIMALS AND WRITTEN WORDS

Elephants don't *wonder* about their trunks
Or try to *understand* the ways of skunks.
Lions don't tell stories or tear down
Jungle walls to *make* way for a town.
Tigers never *decorate* a house.
Leopards *show* no mercy for the mouse.
The fox in hunger pouncing on his prize
Learns nothing from a frightened rabbit's eyes.
None ever *plowed* a field or *planted* grain,
Or *bound* a wound or *healed* another's pain,
Or *broke* with stones the casing of the corn,
Or *sang* to heaven when a child was born.

Least of them all, far frailer than the fawn,
Early man was ill to look upon;
Hairy, with clawed hands and flung-down head
He groped for remnants after lions fed.

[16] Arthur Razzell and K. G. O. Watts, *Probability: The Science of Chance*, pp. 3–5.

Prey of all things man slept in trees at first,
Hungered, frightened and consumed with thirst.
Keen to his scent, below him prowled the beast,
Awaiting dawn and the primeval feast.

Inside man's skull a torment no other creature knew,
A pendulum swinging and crying: "This is false! This is
    true!"
"You can think . . . and choose . . . and plan . . .
These are the magic qualities of MAN!
Lift up your head, for you alone can reason,
And master every problem in its season."

Man struck at first with clubs, and later stones,
And draped his neck with white, black-panther bones.
No other thing before had won a fight
By *using weapons* to increase its might.
Fear lessened, food increased, dream and desire
Broke cold and darkness: Man discovered fire!

How long between the hurled stone and the rose?
A million years? Nobody really knows.
From tools and drawings on old walls and rock
Man's history begins: a picture-clock.
The hands move slowly, driven by the mind
Toward abstract thoughts and, striking noon, they find
Reason's symbols sounding left and right—
The *alphabet of letters* is in sight!

This backward journey is the way we go
Through all recorded history that we know
To find our English is not old, but young—
And set with jewels from every other tongue![17]

Another poem in the same volume, "The Wonderful
Words," deals with the importance of language to
thought:

[17] Mary O'Neill, *Words, Words, Words,* pp. 8–10.

THE WONDERFUL WORDS

Never let a thought shrivel and die
For want of a way to say it,
For English is a wonderful game
And all of you can play it.
All that you do is match the words
To the brightest thoughts in your head
So that they come out clear and true
And handsomely groomed and fed—
For many of the loveliest things
Have never yet been said.
Words are the food and dress of thought,
They give it its body and swing,
And everyone's longing today to hear
Some fresh and beautiful thing.
But only words can free a thought
From its prison behind your eyes.
Maybe your mind is holding now
A marvelous new surprise![18]

Poems such as these may encourage learners to "sharpen" their language in order to avoid making mistakes in their thinking.

CRITICAL THINKING IN CHILDREN'S FICTION

Learners need to understand that fiction is full of fact, that fiction can be very close to human life and can provide us with rare insights about ourselves and those around us. They need to recognize as well that because fiction is close to life, thinking and the importance of thinking may be reflected quite as much

[18] Mary O'Neill, *op. cit.*, p. 63.

in a novel as in a history of science. In many cases the problems faced and solved by characters in works of fiction seem closer to learners because the learners recognize the problems as similar to *their* problems.

Some classic "problem-solvers" in fiction, whom most learners meet in the course of growing up, are Tom Sawyer and Huckleberry Finn. On almost any page of either *The Adventures of Tom Sawyer* or *The Adventures of Huckleberry Finn* the reader finds the heroes faced with some difficulty which they must overcome. Some of these problems are solved intelligently and some are simply bumbled through. (For the heroes to solve *all* of their problems intelligently would make them seem something less than real boys.) The following passage describes an incident from *Huckleberry Finn* in which Huck uses critical thinking to solve a problem. He wants to escape from his father and make both his father and Widow Douglas believe that he has been killed.

About twelve o'clock we turned out and went along up the bank. The river was coming up pretty fast, and lots of driftwood going by on the rise. By and by, along comes part of a log raft—nine logs fast together. We went out with the skiff and towed it ashore. Then we had dinner. Anybody but pap would a waited and seen the day through, so as to catch more stuff; but that warn't pap's style. Nine logs was enough for one time; he must shove right over to town and sell. So he locked me in and took the skiff and started off towing the raft about half-past three. I judged he wouldn't come back that night. I waited till I reckoned he had got a good start, then I out with my saw and went to work on that log again. Before he was t'other side of the river I was out of the hole; him and his raft was just a speck on the water away off yonder.

I took the sack of corn meal and took it to where the canoe was hid, and shoved the vines and branches apart and put it in; then I done the same with the side of bacon; then the whisky jug; I took all the coffee and sugar there was, and all the ammunition; I took the wadding; I took the bucket and gourd; I took a dipper and a tin cup, and my old saw and two blankets, and the skillet and the coffee-pot. I took fishlines and matches and other things—everything that was worth a cent. I cleaned out the place. I wanted an ax, but there wasn't any, only the one out at the woodpile, and I knowed why I was going to leave that. I fetched out the gun, and now I was done.

I had wore the ground a good deal, crawling out of the hole and dragging out so many things. So I fixed that as good as I could from the outside by scattering dust on the place, which covered up the smoothness and the sawdust. Then I fixed the piece of log back into its place, and put two rocks under it and one against it to hold it there—for it was bent up at that place, and didn't quite touch ground. If you stood four or five foot away you didn't know it was sawed, you wouldn't ever notice it; and besides, this was the back of the cabin and it warn't likely anybody would go fooling around there.

It was all grass clear to the canoe; so I hadn't left a track. I followed around to see. I stood on the bank and looked out over the river. All safe. So I took the gun and went up a piece into the woods and was hunting around for some birds, when I see a wild pig; hogs soon went wild in them bottoms after they had got away from the prairie farms. I shot this fellow and took him into camp.

I took the ax and smashed in the door—I beat it and hacked it considerable, a-doing it. I fetched the pig in and took him back nearly to the table and hacked into his throat with the ax, and laid him down on the ground to bleed—I say ground, because it *was* ground—hard packed, and no boards. Well, next I took an old sack and put a lot of big rocks in it—all I could drag—and I started it from the pig and dragged it to the door and through the woods down to the river and dumped it in, and down it sunk, out of sight. You could easy see that something had been dragged over the ground. I did wish Tom Sawyer was there, I knowed he would take an interest in this kind of business, and throw in the fancy touches.[19]

Learners will see in these books that even though Huck and Tom are not highly educated in any formal sense, they have developed and use many of the skills of critical thinking.

Sometimes when we talk to learners about problem-solving we may give them the impression that as they tackle problems the process will go smoothly. We know, of course, that things seldom work that way; that in solving problems there are false starts, frustrations and mistakes. Part of critical thinking, we must make clear, is to learn from our mistakes as well as from our successes. This point is made in a delightful way in Agnes McCarthy's *Room 10,* a book about a third-grade class and their teacher, Miss Lavender. Miss Lavender encourages the class to solve their problems and allows them to make mistakes and to learn from those mistakes. The following section from the book is one instance of this.

Right after Thanksgiving, Miss Lavender said, "We must think about what to do for the holidays. Shall we have a party for the parents?"

We all said, "Yes!"

"Fine," said Miss Lavender. "What shall we do at the party?"

[19] Mark Twain, *The Adventures of Huckleberry Finn,* pp. 47–49.

"We can have cookies and cupcakes," said Richard.

"We should have lemonade or cocoa," said Sharon.

We boys began to get hungry.

"Well, what should we do besides eat?" asked Miss Lavender.

"Let's give a play," said Millie.

Some boys made faces at her. Others smiled. Most of us thought a play was a good idea.

Miss Lavender said, "Now you should decide what your play will be about. And you should think about the characters—the people—in the play. I'll write your ideas on the chalkboard."

"I think the play should be about winter," said Dick Dirkie.

"And Christmas," said Millie.

"And Chanukah," said Arlene.

"And we should have Santa Claus in the play," said Jimmy.

"Also, a few angels," said Sharon.

"And some winter sports, like skiing," I said.

"Don't forget the Wise Men," said Richard.

"Or the menorah," said Arlene.

Miss Lavender was writing like mad. The chalk was getting short.

"It would be cute to have a few elves," said Laurie.

"And shepherds and lambs," I added.

When we finished telling our ideas, we looked at the list. It covered the whole chalkboard, even under the map of the United States.

"Now," said Miss Lavender, "you can choose from the list. Choose the ideas you like best. Then you can make a play using just those ideas."

We all looked at the list.

I said, "I like all the ideas."

Richard said, "I do, too."

Most of us liked all the ideas.

"Let's put them all in the play," said Dick Dirkie.

"That would be hard to do," said Miss Lavender. "How can you make a play about all these things? How could you fit them all in? How could you make all the costumes? I think you had better choose just a few things."

Some of us groaned.

Laurie stood up. She said, "Miss Lavender, we'd like to try a play with everything in it."

Miss Lavender didn't say anything for a minute. Then she said, "All right. I'll let you have a few days to work on a play like that. If you find that it won't work, let me know. Then we can plan again."

That afternoon we made ourselves into different groups. Some of us were in the playwriting group. Others were in the costume group. I was in the scenery group with Dick Dirkie and Richard.

"For Santa Claus we need a chimney," said Richard. He wrote CHIMNEY.

"For the shepherds we need a hill and some fake sheep," I said.

"For winter sports we need a hill and a ski tow," said Dick Dirkie.

"We can use the same hill for the shepherds and the ski tow," said Richard.

"That's silly," I said. "The shepherds of those days didn't have ski tows."

"Don't forget the chimney for Santa Claus," said Richard.

We all groaned slightly. We were glad when the recess bell rang.

At recess we talked to the costume group.

"How is the costume group doing?" I asked Laurie.

"Well, we're having some trouble," said Laurie. "We think it will look funny for the Wise Men to have robes, and for the elves to have little green hats, and all be on the stage together."

"We'll find a way," said Millie.

Sharon came over. She said, "How is the scenery group doing?"

"Not so good," Richard said. "How is the playwriting group?"

"We're trying to think of a conversation that Santa Claus could have with an angel," said Sharon. "That's our big problem right now."

"Don't tell Miss Lavender that we're having trouble," said Laurie. "We told her we wanted this kind of play. Now we must make it work."

"Don't kid yourself," I said. "Miss Lavender already *knows* we're having trouble. I saw her smiling sadly at us."

"We'll practice and practice," said Dick Dirkie. "Even after school."

We all sighed. But that was the truth. That was what we had to do. We wanted to prove to Miss Lavender that we could do it.

Every day after school we practiced and practiced.

Every day Miss Lavender said, "Would you like to plan another kind of play?"

"No, Miss Lavender," we said. "We like our play. It's coming along."

"May I help you in any way?" said Miss Lavender.

"No, Miss Lavender," said Sharon. "We want the play to be a surprise for you, too."

"Oh," said Miss Lavender. "Well, I'm sure it will be."

One day, about two days before we had to give the play, we were practicing in Millie's house. Everything was rather bad. Everything was confusing. The costumes were tearing. The scenery was falling down. Nobody knew his part. Then sometimes, the stage got so crowded that people bumped into one another. Elves and skiers and Wise Men were all over the place at one time, all talking at once.

"This is very bad," said Sharon.

"We need a little help," said Dick Dirkie.

"Who shall we ask?" I said.

We all looked at each other.

"We should ask Miss Lavender," said Richard.

So the next day, we did.

Miss Lavender listened to our problem very sweetly. She didn't say *I told you so*. She didn't say *You should have listened to me*. Miss Lavender isn't like that. She said, "Well, the play is tomorrow. We've invited the parents. There must be *some* kind of play . . ."

"Ours is awful," said Millie.

"Tell me," said Miss Lavender. "Why did you want a play with so many characters and ideas in it?"

"Because they are all a part of Chanukah and Christmas," said Dick Dirkie.

"Christmas and Chanukah have so many parts to them," said Sharon.

"You could tell the parents that," said Miss Lavender. "You could tell them about the many parts of the holidays."

"Would that be a play?" asked Richard.

"If we wore our costumes," said Laurie. "It would be a play if we wore our costumes."

"That's right," said Jimmy. "We'll fix our costumes. Then each person will tell how he is a part of the holidays."

"That's a good idea!" said Laurie.

I said, "Whew!" We all stopped being worried. We practiced our new parts all day. We didn't worry about scenery. Miss Lavender didn't make us do arithmetic or reading. At the end of the day, we felt good about our play. We could hardly wait for the party.

The parents liked the play. Each child came out in a costume. The Wise Men told how they brought gifts on the first Christmas long ago. The Santa Claus told how he brings gifts to children nowadays. The menorah candle told how the lamps burned for eight days on the first Chanukah. The skiers told how they ski down hills in winter. The shepherds told about the cold snow on the hills near Bethlehem.

Everyone clapped when the play was over. Then we had refreshments. Then the parents went home.

While we were cleaning up, Richard said to Miss Lavender, "That was fun."

Laurie said, "Let's give another play on Valentine's Day."

Miss Lavender held her head.

"What shall we have in it?" said Millie.

"Valentines," said Dick Dirkie.

"And cupids," said Sharon.

"And postmen delivering valentines," said Jimmy.

"And people making valentines," I said.

"Wait, wait!" said Richard. "We're forgetting something."

We all stopped and thought for a minute. Then we laughed.

"*This* time," said Millie, "we had better have just a *few* things in our play."

Miss Lavender smiled. Then she said, "We had better finish cleaning the room."[20]

The children in Miss Lavender's class *have* solved a problem. They have discovered what will work, but only after testing something which does not work. We can help our own learners recognize that they too have learned many things from their mistakes.

Earlier we commented that we often tend to jump to conclusions, to decide that something is the case even though the evidence is clearly inadequate. It is probably easier for us to recognize this tendency in other people than in ourselves, and easier for learners to see it in the characters they read about than in their

[20] Agnes McCarthy, *Room 10,* pp. 35–37, 40–43.

own behavior. And one set of characters in which learners will recognize this problem is found in another book by Agnes McCarthy, *The Impossibles*. This story tells of the adventures of a group of neighborhood boys, The Secret Agents, and the neighborhood girls, the Girls' Friendliness and Helpful Club. The first experience of The Secret Agents is a good example. After looking at the "Wanted" posters in the post office, the boys conclude that a stranger seen in the local hardware store is one of the fugitives:

"What should we do now?" said George Feather.

"We'd better get our secret equipment ready," said Kim. We went around in back of Pink's Hardware. We put on some disguises from George's kit.

"This way we can follow Henry Lemon without being noticed," said Royston Oyster.

We went around to the front of the store and waited.

Henry Lemon came out. He started toward Lacey's Drugstore. We followed him very slowly, right into the drugstore. Henry Lemon went up to the counter and ordered a cup of coffee from Mr. Lacey. We all sat on stools near the bad guy. We pretended we were not together.

"In town for long?" said Mr. Lacey to Henry Lemon.

"No," said Henry Lemon. "Just passing through."

Royston Oyster gave me a little nudge with his elbow. "Did you hear that?" he whispered.

"Where are you staying?" said Mr. Lacey.

"The usual place," said Henry Lemon.

"Probably a hideout," I whispered to Royston.

"How does the town look to you?" said Mr. Lacey.

"Pretty good," said Henry Lemon.

"He means pretty good to rob," said Royston Oyster.

Just then Mrs. Costello came into the drugstore. She came right over to us. "Why, boys!" she said. "How cute you look in your disguises!"

"Aw, gee, Mom!" said Kim. He was mad. His mustache fell off slightly.

Henry Lemon turned and looked at us. "Aren't you the boys I saw in the hardware store?" he said.

I gulped. "Oh, no," I said. "We never go in hardware stores. Never."

"Well, it's time to go," said Mrs. Costello. She made us all go back to the car with her. We didn't say much on the way home.

"Why are you boys so grumpy?" said Mrs. Costello.

"Our feet are a little cold," said Kim.

When we got home, we all went into George Feather's kitchen. His mother made us some cocoa. When she left, George said, "I think we'd better quit trying to catch Henry Lemon. I think he may be getting a little angry."

"Secret Agents are supposed to be brave," I said.

"There are four of us and one of him," said Royston.

"We have to help our town," said Kim. "Henry Lemon is a bad guy."

"Well," said George, "maybe we should get some grownup to help us. It doesn't do much good just to follow Henry Lemon around wearing disguises."

"That's true," said Royston Oyster. "Besides, Henry Lemon knows who we are now, even with disguises. He knows we're watching him."

"I hope he doesn't try to seek revenge against us," said George Feather.

Just then Mr. Feather came in. My father was with him. They had been out ice-fishing.

"Well, Johnny," said my dad, "what have you boys been up to today?"

"We've had a bad day, Dad," I said.

"We've been chasing a crook, Mr. MacIntyre," said Royston Oyster. "A crook named Henry Lemon."

"Is that so?" said my dad. "Tell us about it." So my dad and Mr. Feather sat down and we told them all about the bad guy and how we'd followed him and how we saw him steal nails and how we'd heard his bad-guy conversation in the drugstore.

"It's all part of our new secret-agent club," said Kim Costello.

"And you're sure this man is Henry Lemon?" said my dad.

"Positive," said Royston Oyster.

"He's small, and has green eyes, and does sneaky things," I said. "Just like the post office sign said."

The doorbell rang. Mrs. Feather went to the door.

There was Henry Lemon! I nearly fell off my chair.

"He's come to get us!" yelled George Feather.

"Save us!" said Kim Costello.

Royston Oyster didn't say anything. His eyes just got big.

"My goodness! What a surprise!" said Mrs. Feather to Henry Lemon. She said to Mr. Feather, "Honey, come see who's dropped in!"

Mr. Feather went to the door. "Why, Randy Pink!" he said. "When did you get back in town?"

"Randy Pink?" I whispered to Royston. "He looks like Henry Lemon to me."

"Come in here," said Mr. Feather to Randy Pink-Henry Lemon. "I want you to meet my son George and his friends. You've been away so long that you've never met our gang of boys."

Randy Pink-Henry Lemon came into the kitchen. Our faces got slightly red.

"Boys," said Mr. Feather, "this is Randy Pink, the son of Mr. Pink of Pink's Hardware."

"Oh . . . ," we all said very softly. Then we said, "Hello."

"I believe I saw these boys down in the village today," said Randy Pink. "They were wearing disguises."

"That's true," said Royston Oyster. Then he pretended to be drinking cocoa.

"Randy's in the Merchant Marine," said my father.

"He sails all around the world. He doesn't get back home very often." I looked at my dad, and he looked at me. I noticed that my dad had a slight smile in his eyes.

"Well, it's good to be home for a while," said Randy Pink. "It was good to help my dad in the store today. I sorted nails for him. And it was good to chat with Mr. Lacey at the drugstore, too."

Mrs. Feather said, "Come up and see our new baby, Randy." Randy went off to the baby's room.

Then George said, "Randy Pink has brown eyes, not green ones."

Kim Costello said, "Randy Pink is a little taller than five feet."

Royston Oyster said, "I still think he looks just like Henry Lemon."

"Now, Royston," said my dad, "it's impossible for one person to be two people at once."

"That's true," said Royston Oyster. "This has been an impossible day."

"Maybe you should call yourselves The Impossibles instead of The Secret Agents," said Mr. Feather. He and my dad started to laugh.

Our feelings got slightly hurt.[21]

Most learners will recall instances in their own lives when they have drawn hasty conclusions which they later regretted. Sometimes critical thinking should lead us to reserve judgment rather than to draw a conclusion.

Many excellent examples of critical thinking are found in mystery stories. One such story is Edward Fenton's *The Riddle of the Red Whale*. In this book the teen-age heroes and their friend and neighbor Mr. Vanniver try to get to the bottom of a series of mysteri-

[21] Agnes McCarthy, *The Impossibles*, pp. 7–11.

ous events in their rural community in upstate New York. In the beginning their only clue is the phrase "red whale." Learners will find this an exciting story, but in addition they will find that it exemplifies the difficulties of solving problems on the basis of evidence which is both sketchy and indirect. In the following passage the main character discusses some of these difficulties:

Obie, as I could tell, was dotting his t's and crossing his i's, applying scientific methods to the already known facts. For my part, I was reflecting that, for all any of us knew, the red whale might be near at hand. Perhaps it was under our very eyes. Maybe it was so close that we could practically reach out to touch it if we only had the right key to turn, as it were, or knew which door to open.

It's easy enough for the detectives in books. They always know. The clues are so easy to follow. All they have to do is stand off and look at them from a slightly different angle and everything just slips into focus. "Elementary, my dear Dr. Watson!" Or else the criminals are obliging enough to leave notes behind with cryptic rhymes, or a significant word scrawled across a mirror with a lipstick. It's no wonder Sherlock Holmes and Albert Campion and Hercule Poirot and all the others turn out to be so clever in the end!

If only it was as easy as that in real life. Trying to get at the actual facts, I told myself ruefully, was like trying to catch guppies with your bare fingers.[22]

Learners will recognize this sort of difficulty in solving many of the problems which they face. Problems which are very easily solved hardly seem to be problems at all.

[22] Edward Fenton, *The Riddle of the Red Whale,* pp. 145–46.

It is probably natural for children, as well as adults, to try to solve with brute strength some of the problems they have with other people. This is especially true for many children who are large for their age and are teased about their size, as happens to Veronica in Marilyn Sachs's *Veronica Ganz*. But, as many have learned before her, Veronica finds that some problems require more thought than action:

"I'm thinking!" Veronica shouted.

"Oh," Stanley said, "that's what you've been busy doing all day—thinking."

But Stanley was mistaken. Veronica had not been thinking all day, but now she was, and her mind creaked and groaned under its burden. Stanley stood looking up at her tormented face. "Veronica," he whimpered, "let's go home, Veronica."

But Veronica didn't hear him. She was fighting a hard battle now, and her adversary was herself. Peter Wedemeyer had eluded her and outfoxed her down the line. It wasn't enough that she was stronger than he. If she couldn't outsmart him, the victory would be his. She was going to need a new weapon to beat Peter, and that weapon lay somewhere inside her own brain. If she couldn't find it, then it was all over for her, and Peter could go on teasing and tormenting her forever and ever, and she'd never be able to stop him. Was there any point in going on with this contest, which served only to humiliate her time and again? Should she admit that Peter was just too much for her—too smart for her? Should she forget the whole business, and keep out of his way? Or should she try again?

"I'm cold," Stanley whimpered. "I want to go home."

"In a minute, in a minute," she muttered, because there was something bursting into light inside her brain. A trap. Of course. A trap. She'd lay a trap. She'd beat him at his own game, and show him that she was as good as he, and twice as smart. She'd lay a trap for him that he'd walk right into. And how easy it all would be.[23]

Of course, Veronica learns that finding the solution to her problem is not so easy. But she also learns many other things as she finds out that methods she has used to overcome her problems in the past no longer work. Preteen girls will find that they share some of Veronica's problems.

Many children have encountered difficulties much like those faced by David Keegan in Eileen Rosenbaum's *Two for Trouble*. The "two" in this case are stray kittens who have adopted David. David's major problem centers around the fact that, due to his mother's allergies, he must find homes for the kittens. After he has tried and failed with conventional methods—such as knocking on doors and asking people if they'd like a kitten—he begins to think about more novel schemes. One of these is described in the section below:

David waited for his aunt outside of Costa's. When she finally came out, he had a few questions to ask her. "Did you really mean it when you said you can give away *anything* if you raffle it?" he asked, as they tramped back up the hill, David loaded to the eyeballs with little green bags from the fruit market.

"Absolutely!" she declared. "Of course, it helps if it's all for a good cause. Then people can assure themselves they're being quite unselfish. Why, what in creation would Daisy Krantz do with a car? When I knew her, she couldn't even ride a bicycle!"

David unloaded the bags on the kitchen table and, with-

23 Marilyn Sachs, *Veronica Ganz*, pp. 101, 103.

out waiting to see what was inside, rushed off to Snooper's house.

"Hey, Snooper, what's a good cause?" he asked, after forcing Snooper away from his back fence where he had been spying on the neighbors.

"Huh?" Snooper hooted, annoyed at the interruption.

"What's a good cause?" David repeated.

"I don't get you!" Snooper's nose wrinkled.

"Like—if you were a grownup—what would you think would need fixing or changing in the world?"

"Taxes!" Snooper said promptly. "Grownups complain a lot about taxes. Like school taxes and stuff. Every time I bring home a report card, my dad waves it around and shouts about how much my 'Cs' are costing him. I'm not sure exactly what he means, but I keep thinking that if taxes were lower, he wouldn't be so mad about my grades."

It made sense to David. He had heard his father say that school taxes had been skyrocketing in the past few years. "So that would be a good cause—bringing down school taxes. Right?"

Snooper nodded positively. "Right!"

"And if I collected a whole lot of money and gave it to Mr. Candless to pay for—uh—books and desks and stuff, that would make taxes lower, right?"

Snooper, anxious to get back to his spying, was no longer paying attention. "I guess so," he said with a shrug.

"It's settled, then!" David turned to rush away. "Don't forget you promised to keep the kittens until Saturday!" he called over his shoulder.[24]

Throughout the book the reader finds David devising plans to find homes for the kittens. Many of his schemes fail, but his imagination and persistence triumph in the end. David's approaches to his problem

[24] Eileen Rosenbaum, *Two for Trouble,* pp. 95–96.

may seem far out to many learners, but his problem, they will see, is a real one.

One way to make clear how important problem-solving is in our everyday life is to imagine what would happen if we were *not* able to solve even small problems. And for a delightful treatment of an imaginary family whose members are inept in thinking through even the most trivial problem, we have Lucretia P. Hale's *The Peterkin Papers*. The Peterkin family, faced with the smallest difficulty, turns to the lady from Philadelphia for the solution. The book is filled with accounts of problems the Peterkin family must have help to solve, problems which we would not view as problems at all. As an example, let us take the case of Agamemnon's invention:

Agamemnon was delayed, however, in his choice of a profession, by a desire he had to become a famous inventor. If he could only invent something important, and get out a patent, he would make himself known all over the country. If he could get out a patent he would be set up for life, or at least as long as the patent lasted, and it would be well to be sure to arrange it to last through his natural life.

Indeed, he had gone so far as to make his invention. It had been suggested by their trouble with a key, in their late moving to their new house. He had studied the matter over a great deal. He looked it up in the Encyclopedia, and had spent a day or two in the Public Library, in reading about Chubb's Lock and other patent locks.

But his plan was more simple. It was this: that all keys should be made alike! He wondered it had not been thought of before; but so it was, Solomon John said, with all inventions, with Christopher Columbus, and everybody. Nobody knew the invention till it was invented, and then it looked very simple. With Agamemnon's plan you need have but one key, that should fit everything! It should be a medium-sized key, not too large to carry. It ought to answer for a house door, but you might open a portmanteau with it. How much less danger there would be of losing one's keys if there were only one to lose!

Mrs. Peterkin thought it would be inconvenient if their father were out, and she wanted to open the jam closet for the little boys. But Agamemnon explained that he did not mean there should be but one key in the family, or in a town—you might have as many as you pleased, only they should all be alike.

Elizabeth Eliza felt it would be a great convenience—they could keep the front door always locked, yet she could open it with the key of her upper drawer; that she was sure to have with her. And Mrs. Peterkin felt it might be a convenience if they had one on each story, so that they need not go up and down for it.

Mr. Peterkin studied all the papers and advertisements, to decide about the lawyer whom they should consult, and at last, one morning, they went into town to visit a patent agent.

Elizabeth Eliza took the occasion to make a call upon the lady from Philadelphia, but she came back hurriedly to her mother.

"I have had a delightful call," she said; "but—perhaps I was wrong—I could not help, in conversation, speaking of Agamemnon's proposed patent. I ought not to have mentioned it, as such things are kept profound secrets; they say women always do tell things; I suppose that is the reason."

"But where is the harm?" asked Mrs. Peterkin. "I'm sure you can trust the lady from Philadelphia."

Elizabeth Eliza then explained that the lady from Philadelphia had questioned the plan a little when it was told her, and had suggested that "If everybody had the same key there would be no particular use in a lock."

"Did you explain to her," said Mrs. Peterkin, "that we were not all to have the same keys?"

"I couldn't quite understand her," said Elizabeth Eliza, "but she seemed to think that burglars and other people might come in if the keys were the same."

"Agamemnon would not sell his patent to burglars!" said Mrs. Peterkin, indignantly.

"But about other people," said Elizabeth Eliza; "there is my upper drawer; the little boys might open it at Christmastime—and their presents in it!"

"And I am not sure that I could trust Amanda," said Mrs. Peterkin, considering.

Both she and Elizabeth Eliza felt that Mr. Peterkin ought to know what the lady from Philadelphia had suggested.[25]

Why do the Peterkins have problems which the rest of us do not have? Learners will see that their past experiences and past thinking give them ready-made solutions to the sort of situation which represents a problem to a Peterkin.

Perhaps fairy tales and myths are not good places to look for examples of critical thinking, but there are exceptions. Robert E. Huldschiner's *The Cow that Spoke for Seppl and Other Alpine Tales* is one such exception. In *The Cow that Spoke for Seppl* the residents of an Alpine village have concluded that either Silent Seppl or his cow can speak. They are further convinced that the one who can speak is extremely wise and can solve the most difficult problems the village faces. However, neither Silent Seppl nor his cow will answer when asked to speak. The villagers decide to solve their problem by taking Seppl and his cow to a judge in a neighboring town. The judge, they are

[25] Lucretia P. Hale, *The Peterkin Papers*, pp. 132–34.

sure, will be able to determine which one speaks. And the judge, being convinced that neither can speak, solves the problem as follows:

He thought for a while. Then he said, "I wish I could keep quiet, too. But I'm a judge and must render judgment and have to talk. You're a peasant and work the fields and don't have to talk."

"Hic," said Seppl.

"Cows don't have to talk either," said the judge.

"Nooohh," said the cow.

"I like you," said the judge. "If people kept quiet the way you do, this would be a much better world to live in. We could all be happy without having to explain why. But we can't tell this to your mayor."

"Hic," said Seppl.

"Nooohh," said the cow, growing frantic with hunger.

"Of course, we can't tell the mayor," nodded the judge. "The village people argue all the time because they like to argue, and if they didn't believe that you can settle their arguments, there would be no end to it. So they must be convinced that you can talk, and it doesn't matter which of you does the talking."

"Hic," said Seppl.

"Nooohh," said the cow, munching on the last daisy in the courtyard.

"I'll get you some hay," said the judge, "and tomorrow you go home."

The next morning the judge sent a messenger to the village and called the mayor. The mayor hurried to town. The village people had not had a good argument or a good night's sleep since Silent Seppl and the cow had gone to jail. It was lonesome without them.

As soon as the mayor appeared before the judge, the judge said, "I have solved your problem."

The mayor smiled broadly and bowed.

"It was a very difficult problem," said the judge.

The mayor beamed. "Our village is an important place and its people have difficult problems," he said.

"You're right," said the judge. "And that's why you're lucky to have two judges right in your village who can solve your problems and settle your arguments."

"Two?" asked the mayor in great surprise.

"Two," nodded the judge. "Both Silent Seppl and his cow have great wisdom, although the cow may have just a little bit more than Seppl."

"Then you spoke to the cow?"

"I did," said the judge firmly.

The mayor jumped up. "May I talk to the cow, too?"

"You certainly may," said the judge amiably. "You are the mayor and would certainly qualify."

"I don't understand," said the mayor.

"It's simple," explained the judge. "The cow will not speak to a person who is not at least as wise as she is. If a man asks her a question and the cow does not answer, it does not mean that the cow cannot speak but that the person who wants to speak to her is stupid."

"I see," said the mayor and sat down.

The judge smiled at him, and the mayor gave him an uncertain smile in return. "You will be glad to take Silent Seppl and his cow back to the village," said the judge.

The mayor nodded vigorously. "The people are waiting," he said.

"Take them home, then," said the judge, "and remember, it isn't every village that can turn to a wise man and a wise cow in time of trouble. Remember also that you should not turn to them except when the questions you have are important enough to call for their counsel. If stupid men ask stupid questions, neither Seppl nor his cow will ever speak again."[26]

[26] Robert E. Huldschiner, *The Cow that Spoke for Seppl*, pp. 24–26.

Given this tale, young learners might be asked to think about *why* the judge would solve the problem this way.

As teachers, we know that sometimes we fail to understand a learner's problem because we tend to see that problem in our own terms rather than his. In Claire Oleson's *For Pepita—an Orange Tree,* we find adults who are unable to solve the problem of finding a birthday gift for Pepita which will make her happy. Pepita *says* she wants an orange tree, but her friends and relatives give her nicer gifts because they are sure that she will soon forget about the orange tree. But her best friend, Manolo, who has no money with which to buy a gift, understands and solves the problem:

"Pepita crying, and on her birthday," he said to himself. "It must not be. I must think of something—*quick.*"

He did, and came to so sudden a stop that poor Angelita all but tumbled over backward. Manolo lifted Pepita down off Angelita's back. "Now you wait here," he told her, "and you too, Angelita."

Then he ran off across the sands and on up the hill to the huge orange orchard that crowned it. He climbed in over the low stone fence and looked around. There on the ground lay an orange. It was not a very nice one—an all-over bruises and bumps one. But, "It will do," murmured Manolo.

He poked in a finger and pulled out a seed. And with the seed clutched tight, he went racing down the hill and straight up to Pepita.

"For you!" he said, and thrust the seed into her hand. He looked very pleased with himself.

Pepita looked puzzled. "For me? An orange seed?" she said.

"Orange *tree,*" shouted Manolo.

Pepita's eyes began to sparkle and then to dance. *"An orange tree,"* she cried. "An orange tree all my very own!"

Carefully, she placed the seed in the small brown shell.[27]

The others were seeing the orange tree from their own perspective. Only Manolo was able to see it as Pepita did. Learners can probably cite for us many instances when adults have failed to understand their problems. Whenever we think we are engaged in mutual problem-solving, it is a good idea to find out if all the problem-solvers are dealing with the same problem. Too often we both fail to help others solve problems they do have, and work hard to solve problems they do not have.

Learners often have the necessary information to solve problems but do not realize they have it. Young children will enjoy sharing Barney's problem in Craig Bettinger's *Follow Me, Everybody*. Barney's class, and their teacher Mrs. Hale, are visiting the zoo. Because Barney is familiar with the zoo and knows a great deal about the animals, he serves as the guide. He leads the class from one animal to another, giving a short but informative talk about each one. When it is time to return to the school bus, however, Barney discovers that he cannot remember the way. Mrs. Hale guides the class back, past each of the animals they have seen and onto the bus. Barney is crestfallen:

"I guess I wasn't a very good guide," I said. "I found my way in but I lost my way out. I wasn't much help to you."

"Of course you were, Barney," Mrs. Hale said. "You were a big help. How do you think I found the way back? I just looked at the animal list you helped me make. It was like a map. I followed from the last animal on the list back

27 Claire Oleson, *For Pepita—an Orange Tree*, pp. 34–36.

to the first. When we got to the giraffes, it was easy to find the bus. It was your animal map that guided us out of the zoo."

I felt much better when I heard that.

All the way back to school we talked about the zoo, and Mrs. Hale promised we could come again.

"And when we do," she said, "you can be sure of one thing, Barney. We'll all follow you."[28]

Barney had the information he needed to find his way back, but he didn't see that the information had to be "turned around" to solve the problem. Young learners could be asked to solve Barney's problem for him at the appropriate point in the book. But the central point for learners to understand is that having the information or evidence to solve a problem is not sufficient; we must also be able to see how the information or evidence is to be used in the solution.

Jim Starling, in E. W. Hildick's *Jim Starling and the Colonel*, faces the problem of proving to a skeptical, retired army colonel that the younger generation is not soft and pampered. In order to convince the Colonel, Jim decides to better the feats of a youth of the Colonel's own generation, feats recorded in an old newspaper and recalled by the Colonel in a speech to Jim's class at the local secondary school. Jim encounters many difficulties in repeating the feats, which include a distance run, a swim in the river, a timed ride on an old-fashioned bicycle, an eating contest, and an egg-juggling performance. Part of Jim's problems are solved by thinking and research rather than by physical prowess. For example, Jim and his friends discover that the record of the distance run from the Weaver's Arms to

[28] Craig Bettinger, *Follow Me, Everybody,* pp. 91, 93.

the Golden Lion in a quarter of an hour is misleading since at the time the record was set the Weaver's Arms was located much closer to the Golden Lion than at present. But even when the old and much shorter path is located, a problem remains. The old path is strewn with stones which will make running difficult if not impossible. How Jim and his friends overcome this obstacle is explained in the following excerpt:

They watched the resultant melee with a mixture of amusement and respect, for no one could help admiring Birdy Willis' powers of imagination and stage management. A thin, sharp-nosed boy, with cross-eyes and a black lens to his glasses, he was in the second year at Cement Street. He didn't get on very well with boys of his own age and he spent most of his time with youngsters, organizing them in gangs and spellbinding them with his bright ideas for giving new life to old games.

He stood there now, surrounded by bristling guns and enjoying two roles: the stagecoach driver who said, "We ain't carryin' the bullion today, ya yeller-bellied thievin' scum!"; and the stage manager who broke off to say, "Then I jump in an' you don't know it's armor-plated an' I've got a machine gun, an' then I get the lotter yer!"

Which he proceeded to do.

Nip's jaw came out scornfully.

"No wonder he only gets *kids* to play with him! Machine guns! In the Wild West! I—"

"Hey! Shurrup a minute! I've just had an idea!"

Terry's eyes were gleaming. He stood on the wall and called out: "Hi, Birdy! What you playin' at now?"

The others groaned.

"What you want to call *him* for? We'll never get rid of him!"

It looked as if Nip was right. Birdy had answered with

a surprised grin and was now walking through the grass
with his gang behind him.

"Wells Fargo!" he said. "This is the stagecoach."

Terry sniffed.

"Wells Fargo! That old stuff! Why don't you think of
summat new?"

Birdy's face flushed. He looked hurt.

"It *is* new . . . It's a change from Cowboys an' Injuns
anyroad . . . I bet *you* couldn't have thought of it!"

Terry sneered.

"*Who* couldn't? You want to play what we're playin'
now if you want summat really new!"

"Hey—we don't—"

Terry brushed Jim's horrified protest aside.

"*Really* new!" he repeated.

Now Birdy was sneering. He seemed very conscious of
the silent gang behind him, who were watching carefully
over their handkerchief masks, curious to see how their
leader would make out in this exchange.

"What? Private Eyes?" he said. "Call *that* new?"

"Nargh!" said Terry. "Brutal Japanese Guards. That's
what we're playin' . . . Brutal Japanese Guards."

Birdy turned his head sideways, the better to focus his
uncovered eye on Terry. His interest was really aroused.
So also were his suspicions.

"What's that?" he asked.

"Like on that picture at the Roxy last week. There's
Brutal Japanese Guards and British Prisoners. We're
reckonin' to build a road across the desert, clearin' away
the rocks an' that, from Burma to—to Alaska."

"Burma to *where*?" began Nip, but Jim shut him up,
suddenly getting the drift of Terry's plan.

"Look," said Terry. "We've done that much already."

Birdy peered over the wall. His eye was gleaming.

"Yer!" he breathed, and they could tell he'd been cap-
tivated by the idea and was already thinking of spicy re-
finements. "Did yer say *we* could play?"

"Well—what d'you say, Jim?"

Jim pretended to consider it.

He stuck out his lips and put his head on one side.

He turned down the corners of his mouth.

He opened his mouth as if to say something, but spat instead.

Then he shrugged.

"Go on, then," he said. "You lot be the Prisoners. We'll be the Brutal Japanese Guards."

"Alyaki! Saki!" came a screech. They turned. If it hadn't been for his ginger hair, Goggles would have looked the part exactly. "To work, dogs!" he howled.

Birdy frowned.

"Just a minute!" he said.

They waited anxiously, wondering if he was going to insist on *his* gang's being the Brutal Japanese Guards.

"I seen that picture too," he said. "An' the men come marchin' to work proper, like the Air Cadets—only whistlin' to show they don't care. All right?"

"Sure!"

"Course!"

"Fine!"

"I mean, they're British, you know. They're the *Goodies.*"

"Yer! Sure! March 'em on, if you like . . . This is where we left off clearin' the road. You can start there."

Birdy nodded, then scowled at his gang.

"All right," he said. "We're gonner show this Japanese shower we got discipline in our mob. Get in threes an' march proper—when I say . . ."

And to the ragged whistling of *Colonel Bogey,* Birdy's brigade took up their working positions under the Brutal Japanese Guards and continued the clearing of the Burma–Alaska Highway. All except Birdy, that is. He found a stick and, carrying it like a swagger cane under his arm, he strolled up and down the line, supervising with the guards.

"I'm the officer," he explained. *"Officers* don't work."[29]

Solving a problem by getting someone else to do the work is, of course, an old theme. Even so, learners can see in this example, and throughout this book, the importance of thinking through problems rather than acting on first impulse.

What, in this day and age, can a subteen do to earn needed money? This is a common problem indeed, and it is the one faced by Jill in Ruth Holberg's *Jill and the Applebird House.* Jill's parents have bought the old Applebird house as a summer home. Before they can clean and redecorate it, Jill's mother is injured in an auto accident and hospitalized. Jill holds herself responsible for the accident and for the mounting expenses. Fearing that her family cannot afford the cost of fixing the summer home, Jill and her friends develop a number of plans to raise money and acquire things needed in the home. One scheme is to bring back the old practice of "swapping":

Jill brought out a pile of ancient newspapers that had made a sort of mat under the carpet. At once she began to read. The print was faded, and most of the yellowed, brittle papers broke into shreds; but one sheet was in better condition.

"Pat! Listen to this! People put ads in the paper under the heading 'Yankee Swappers.' They offered to swap something they wanted to get rid of for something another person didn't need or had too much of. Here's a good one. 'Will swap carriage lanterns for a soapstone sink!'—and another—'I will swap a collection of china cats and hatpins for ladies' clothing and ladies' watches.' "

[29] E. Wallace Hildick, *Jim Starling and the Colonel,* pp. 45–48.

Jill sat on the doorstep reading interesting items from the paper. Her face was dirty and smudged, but her expression was so alert that Pat cried, "Hey, you look as if you'd had a vision!"

Jill looked up. "What an idea I've got! We can gather lots of old things in this house. Then we can get stuff we need in exchange. But we have to think of how to let people know," she muttered to herself while Pat stared at her, equally absorbed in the wonderful idea.

"Hi!" a voice broke in on them. "Hi, Jill. You O.K. now?"

Jill looked blankly at a lanky boy leaning on the fence. Pat said, "It's Tommy Andrews. Don't you know him?"

Jill blushed. "Well, you've grown so tall, Tommy," she explained.

"What in heck are you doing?" he asked, coming into the yard without an invitation and prodding the heap of carpet with his toes. A cloud of dust rose and he sneezed. "You better get rid of this heap of rags." He looked around. "Put it in that old woodshed until the rubbish collector comes."

Jill stood up and Tommy snickered. "You sure look messy. I'll help you. Where's the key to the woodshed?"

Jill didn't have any idea, but it seemed to them that it might be in the rough room, and they galloped up the steps to the upper apartment. Tommy glanced around. "I remember what a time we had last summer during the hurricane."

Jill was poking around hunting for a key. She gave Tommy a grin. "You were so brave and helped me so much. I was scared."

Tommy's face grew red. "Hey, look at this tiny key tied to a bit of wood. Could this be it?"

"Let's try it," Jill said. They tore down the steps, and the key fitted. The door opened on a couple of barrels jammed full with empty tin cans. "Not much room, but

I'll lug in the carpet and stuff it in someplace," offered Tommy.

He went out and pulled in the ragged carpet. Jill poked around the shed. "What's this? An old, dirty kitchen sink?"

Pat said, "That's an old soapstone sink. We got rid of ours years ago, and my mother has it sunk in the garden filled with water and goldfish. They're pretty rare nowadays."

"Hey!" Jill screeched, "that will be our first swap article. And look at this. It has three wheels, a handle, and pedals. Pat, it must be an old-time girl's tricycle. I've seen pictures of them in an old book of children's stories."

Tommy shoved the heap of carpet in a corner and then looked at Jill's treasures. "Maybe there are more junky things." He stood on tiptoe, reached onto a shelf, and lifted down a large school slate. The red felt border was motheaten, but a good slate pencil and a sponge still hung from strings attached to the edge.

Jill cried, "How lucky. We can write the swapping ads on this for people to read, and we can hang it in the store window. And, oh, listen, the store can be the swapping place!"[30]

Jill faces many other problems as the summer proceeds. Some of these she cannot solve by herself, but others she does solve by carefully planning, thinking, and "testing" her plans. And most of the problems Jill faces are problems which, to some extent, face most children of her age.

A very unusual problem appears in Gerry Turner's *Hide-out for a Horse.* This is the story of a little girl's attempts to help the ailing driver of a New York City hansom cab find a place to keep his old horse. Lindy, the little girl, and her friend Harold, face one difficulty

[30] Ruth Holberg, *Jill and the Applebird House,* pp. 19–22.

after another. At one point in the story the carriage
driver, Mr. Kirby, has parked the horse and carriage in
front of the apartment house in which Lindy lives.
Lindy is to watch the horse, Pie, until Mr. Kirby returns from his search for a stable. When it grows late
and Mr. Kirby has not returned, Lindy takes matters
into her own hands:

"Harold, I have an idea." She said it with a strange look
on her face. "I want you to help me sneak Pie up to the
Clubhouse."

"Huh?" The boy stared at her blankly.

"I said we're going to take this horse up on the roof."

"Huh?"

Lindy was already unfastening the straps that held Pie
to the buggy.

"Come on. Help me." She tugged Pie's bridle and led
him onto the sidewalk. "You take off his blanket, Harold,
and cover up Mr. Kirby's stuff with it."

Harold nodded and did as he was told. He looked as if
he were walking in a dream. When the boxes were covered
and Lindy had breathed a silent prayer nothing would be
stolen, she led the horse across the sidewalk and into the
delivery entrance of the apartment house. Harold followed
behind, his eyes wide with fright.

Lindy quickly made her way to the freight elevator. She
stole a glance around and saw that they were alone.

"Hurry up. Open the elevator door," she whispered. The
horse blinked and balked when they tried to push him inside. Lindy gave him another lump of sugar and he meekly
followed her. They closed the door.

"Whew! We made it," Lindy gasped. Then she tried to
reach the elevator button for the top floor, but it was out
of reach. She told Harold to bend down, then climbed on
his back. She finally managed to scramble onto Pie. Leaning forward, she touched the button for the seventeenth

floor. The elevator started up with a groan and shudder. Lindy got off the horse. Harold cringed back, his eyes now big as saucers.

"Gosh!" was all he could say.

The elevator jerked to a stop and Lindy opened the gate. "Come on—push!" she grunted. They moved Pie out onto the landing. There were still a dozen steps to climb to the roof. Pie seemed confused and wouldn't put his legs on the iron staircase.

"Come on, horse," Lindy muttered. She slapped Pie on the rump. He snorted and finally got under way. Each step he took brought a snort or whimper. The sound of his hoofs on the iron steps was terribly loud, booming all the way down the building.

"Jeepers! Hurry up before Mr. Katzmeyer hears us!" Harold wailed. Lindy shuddered at the thought of what the janitor would do if he discovered them. Mr. Katzmeyer had a face like a dried apple. A *crab* apple was more like it, Lindy thought.

At last they reached the roof and Pie went through the door with a last big shove. He crunched over the gravel as they led him across the roof to the Clubhouse.[31]

Lindy's solution proves to be temporary. Even Lindy, with all her drive and imagination, finds it difficult to hide a horse in New York City. But young readers will find in Lindy a problem-solver of the first order.

A sensitive account of how a teen-age boy and those close to him face a serious and difficult moral problem is found in Richard E. Drdek's *The Game.* This is a story about a boy and the uncle with whom he lived in a poor section of Cleveland during the Great Depression. The boy idolizes his uncle and wants to do things for him to make his life easier. The uncle feels

[31] Gerry Turner, *Hide-out for a Horse,* pp. 20–21, 23.

the same way about the boy. The boy finds a box containing a large sum of money and tells his uncle of the discovery and of what the two of them can do with the money. Rather than telling the boy what he ought to do—rather than solving the boy's problem for him, or even telling him that he has a problem—the uncle responds by telling a story. The boy does not immediately see the point of the tale:

There followed a pause during which Sonny patiently waited for his uncle to go on. When he could wait no longer, he asked, "So?"

"So, what?"

"What happened next?"

"I know no more of the story," said the uncle. "Holomecz was never seen or heard from again by any of his friends."

Sonny was silent for a while, and then he asked, "What does it mean?"

"What does what mean?"

Acting exasperated, Sonny explained, "What does the story mean?"

"I'm not sure that it has a meaning. It's just a story told to pass the time away. My great-grandfather knew Holomecz and had heard about the tragedy. It was my great-grandfather who told the story to me when I was a small lad, sitting next to him on the banks of the Uhlava River, fishing."

"Come on now, Unk," the boy entreated. "You know that all of your stories mean something. They have to mean something or you don't tell them."

"A story," said the uncle, "is like a mixed stew. It tastes like whatever the eater thinks it tastes like."

"What you're saying is that I've got to figure it out for myself."

As if he hadn't heard the remark, the uncle asked, "Care for another piece of bread?"[32]

Other characters in the story want to help the boy, but they want to do so by solving his problem for him. The uncle, however, is sure of the boy—so sure that he wants him to think through his problem and decide for himself what he ought to do. There are many lessons which learners might draw from this book. One of these may be that a person may never learn to solve his problems if someone else is always solving them for him: One learns to solve problems only by solving them.

[32] Richard E. Drdek, *The Game*, pp. 51–52.

The Alternatives of Methodology

There is at least one area of decision-making in which the problems that confront the teacher are similar to the ones that confront any creative person: the alternatives of tradition and creativity. In the realm of the playwright, for example, Thornton Wilder once said, "There is something mysterious about the endowment of the storyteller. . . . It springs not, as some have said, from an aversion to general ideas, but from an instinctive coupling of idea and illustration; the idea, for the born storyteller, can only be expressed imbedded in its circumstantial illustration."[1]

He further reasoned that there were effective playwrights and novelists and bad playwrights and novelists, that some of the poorer ones were still revered, while some of the better ones were appreciated only many years after their deaths. The same statements may be made about teachers. Certainly, it is true that the good teacher is able to couple ideas and illustrations. This is necessary in applying theory to practice, and most effective teachers are those who can apply most effectively. Certainly, the best teachers are not always immediately appreciated; neither are the poor ones necessarily discovered at once.

At some point—usually early in his career, however—the playwright must decide to be either a creative or a traditional craftsman. This is also true in the case of

[1] Thornton Wilder, "Some Thoughts on Playwriting," *The Intent of the Artist,* Augusto Centeno, ed. (Princeton, New Jersey: Princeton University Press, 1941), pp. 83–98.

the teacher. If either of these two are willing to pay the price of experimentation to gain true creativity, then this is the direction their careers will take. The price may be one of being misunderstood, it may mean sleepless nights, it may mean lack of financial success, and all of these prices may go for naught upon the discovery that he is a rather poor creative playwright or teacher.

On the other hand, a decision may be made that he is unfit mentally, physically, or emotionally to become creative. He then takes the traditional path. Here there is the risk of boredom with the job, but there is no question that the traditional playwright and teacher are important contributors to our civilization, since it is the traditionalist who passes on the creative efforts of others.

CREATIVITY

Let us consider the creative playwright. There are, of course, effective and ineffective plays of a creative nature. For purposes of this discussion, it must be assumed that effectiveness has some, but not a great deal of, connection with immediate critical success. In this country, the artisan most often cited as an example of an effective playwright is Eugene O'Neill. His use of the allegory in such works as *The Hairy Ape* and *The Great God Brown,* his return to the Greek theater chorus and masks, his experimentation with the length of his plays, and many other effects that he used, mark him as a creative playwright. In addition to all of this, he wrote fine plays. Clearly, here was a successful creative playwright.

On the other hand, *R. U. R.* is, unfortunately, an example of a creative play that is rather ineffective. Whether this play by the Czechoslovakian Karel Čapek suffers in translation, or has naturally trite dialogue, is not important. However, it stands as a play with an unusual theme (at least unusual for 1923) that turns out to be little better than a soap opera in translation. Man's self-destruction through automation was, and is, an important theme for a play, and the setting was most unusual, but the play was not effective. This is not to say that ineffective creative playwrights are not important in our society, because their work may lead the way for effective creative drama or effective traditional drama. The point here is, "Can the individual playwright content himself with being second-rate, or should he attempt to become a first-rate traditionalist?"

The same choice confronts the teacher. If he decides to become a creative person by teaching learners to think, can he be content with being second-rate? He may take the long view that teaching something important, however poorly, is better than not teaching it at all, or he may conclude that teaching something poorly may do harm to the learner. Obviously, the final decision must be left to his conscience. He should be aware, though, that being creative is important, whether one is effective or not.

TRADITIONALISM

Being traditional in an effective manner is also important, however. Our culture would certainly be the poorer if there were no *Blithe Spirit,* no *Arsenic and*

Old Lace. Coward and Crouse and Lindsay chose to present their messages and entertain the audience through conventional, traditional means. Whether they decided this through choice, chance, or a deep-seated knowledge that they were not creative theatrical pioneers does not matter. We are the richer because they wrote their dramas. The traditional teacher, likewise, is able to teach effectively. He can be the follower, the gadfly, or the transmitter. Our society would suffer without the effective traditional teacher.

The only type of playwright or teacher who has no place in our theaters and schools is the ineffective traditional person. This type should probably seek employment elsewhere. There is no excuse for plays such as *Grandpa Goes to Town,* however easy they might be for high-school students to present. There is no literary value here, either creative or traditional. By the same token, we should not have to put up with an ineffective traditional teacher.

THE ALTERNATIVES

The basic difference between the creative and the traditional person is that the creative playwright and teacher stress synthesis—inductive reasoning—the exploration and discovery of new fields, new ideas, new principles. The traditionalist, on the other hand, stresses analysis—deductive reasoning—the refinement of previously discovered fields, ideas, and principles. One cannot do both at the same time; therefore a choice must be made.

There is no doubt that to be effective as a creator or as a traditionalist may require some exclusive talents and abilities. The unfortunate situation exists, though, that many teachers have not made a choice. They have not tried both methods. Most playwrights have tried both; some have been successful at both. But teachers tend to continue in one path without trying the other. We need more teachers to attempt a feat similar to O'Neill's, when he wrote *Ah Wilderness!,* a successful traditional play, in the midst of a long line of experimental, creative dramas.

The real purpose of this chapter, then, is first to urge the traditional teacher to try to be creative through teaching learners to think critically, to present some of the difficulties and pitfalls in this procedure, and then to ask the teacher, "Do you have the desire and the ability to teach creatively?"

THE CHARACTERISTICS OF THE CREATIVE TEACHER

Before a teacher can make a decision regarding creativity, it would be profitable if he were to investigate the attitudes and characteristics of the creative person. For those who have already decided that they want to become creative and have not been too successful in their creative teaching, a consideration of these qualities is also imperative.

Sensitivity. The creative teacher is sensitive to others. He must be aware of the problems of youth, and aware of the physical, emotional, and mental characteristics of youth, especially those characteristics of the group that he teaches. He must also be sensitive to his learners as people with unique characteristics and problems. Only through this sensitivity to his learners can he become sensitive to the problems that are meaningful to them, and only then can he become sensitive to the types of methodology, techniques, and evaluation that are most applicable to his class.

Once he becomes sensitive to all of the above items, he will begin to become aware of the problems of his subject matter that parallel the problems and motivations of his class. At this point, he becomes a person with an almost instinctive ability to couple ideas and illustration—in short, he becomes creative.

Helpfulness. The creative teacher is helpful in his dealings with learners. In the pursuit of knowledge, the learner in the class of the creative teacher is quite likely to come across many frustrations, since he, the learner, must be his own deriver of information. These frustrations are of two kinds: necessary and unnecessary. The necessary ones must be treated by the teacher as normal adjuncts of learning—the anxieties without which no learning would take place. The unnecessary ones must be diagnosed by the teacher as unnecessary, and the learners must then be helped out of their difficulties. For example, if the learner feels that a given experiment will take too much time, yet is within his abilities, the teacher must realize that the learner is not properly motivated, and must be helpful in motivating him—not, however, to the extent that he solves his problem for him.

On the other hand, if the learner has trouble with an investigation that is clearly beyond his capacity, the teacher must be helpful in directing the learner to sources of information, even to the point of letting him solve his problem through the method of testimony, since the learner is not capable of solving it through the method of critical thinking. Furthermore, the creative teacher is always ready to give suggestions on isolating problems or hypotheses, collecting and analyzing data, drawing conclusions, and modifying behavior, based upon the conclusions drawn.

Patience. The creative teacher is patient. He, too, will be confronted by frustrations. If his creative teaching is truly successful, these frustrations will be of a different nature than those confronting the traditional teacher. They will be frustrations of keeping silent in the face of stupidity rather than frustrations of collecting homework papers, but they are there in equal numbers. He must be patient while the learners struggle with new ideas, behave clumsily in their first efforts to perform experiments to synthesize theories, draw incorrect conclusions based upon faulty cause-and-effect relationships, and retrogress to inferior methods of thinking when they are confronted with a frustration.

Honesty. The creative teacher is honest. He must be sure that the learners have all possible facts and principles at hand before they draw conclusions, even though they may lead the learners to unpopular results. He must not let his emotional biases stand in the way of exploring all questions. Finally, he must be honest enough to tell the learners that some areas of investigation, at a certain point in time and space, are not profitable.

Open-mindedness. The creative teacher is open-minded. He must be willing to modify his own thinking or behavior when confronted with tentative proof that he has been mistaken. He must also be tolerant of the thinking of others, since he knows that all questions are pertinent and all answers are tentative in critical exploration.

Observation. The creative teacher is observant. He

must be aware of the actions of learners in order to diagnose those actions as indications of motivation, abilities, and behaviors. He must also be observant in order to be aware of trouble spots in the learner's investigations. Has he selected a problem that will lead only to unnecessary frustration? Is there a possibility that his experiment will have some physical danger connected with it?

Knowledge. The creative teacher is well-informed. He must know his subject matter and have a command of the subject matter of other areas of the curriculum that impinge upon his own subject. In the case of the self-contained classroom teacher, this is obvious, but in the case of the teacher in the departmentalized school, it is equally important. The days are long gone, for example, when the scientist paid no attention to the social implications of his work, when the writer need know no historical facts, or when the geographer needed to know no mathematics.

The teacher must also be informed about his methodology. Learners who are discovering for themselves and behaving as practitioners can have much freedom. Indeed, poor methodology in this situation may snuff out the light of discovery. The teacher must know a great deal about the use of audiovisual equipment as an aid in testing hypotheses or seeking information about a problem, and he must be well-informed in the area of semantics, since communication is so important in teaching creatively.

Finally, he must know his community—its resources or lack of them. He must know the experts of the community, the library, the industries, and all other aspects of the city that may be of some help in supplying information or facilities to be used in the critical thinking of the student.

When all of the above are incorporated into a sensible teacher, we will find that we have a person who would probably do an outstanding job of being a creative teacher. Moreover, if the teacher has all of these characteristics, a subtle change will occur in the student population of his room. The learners will begin to emulate him, to respond to these qualities, and finally to incorporate them into their own lives. All teachers should answer this question: "Do I have these qualities and am I willing to work to become creative?"

A Charge

Dr. T. O. Yntema, a vice-president of the Ford Motor Company, once made a plea that could be accepted as a challenge by creative teachers everywhere:

What we in business want from our schools is people who can do more than report facts and parrot theories and tilt with hypothetical windmills. We need people who can deal with real problems—problems quite theoretical and abstract, and problems often beset by confusing factors and economic limitations. We need people who can see and solve problems and who can cooperate and communicate with others in the process.

Most . . . students are expected to learn facts and theories and techniques. They are expected to apply their theories to cases. But they are hardly ever expected to discover a problem or ask an original question. I am not quite sure how we can get people to learn invention—but I am sure it is possible.[1]

What can be done to help learners develop the habit of critical thinking? There are several action patterns that the creative teacher might well adopt as his own.

[1] T. O. Yntema, in a speech to the 14th Annual Conference on Higher Education at the University of Michigan, Ann Arbor. Reported in the Lansing (Michigan) *State Journal*, November 18, 1961.

BE SELECTIVE

Many, if not most, of the problems that arise in the classroom are not worthy of the method of critical thinking. Obviously, a problem such as "Where is the wastebasket?" is one of these. Less obvious, perhaps, is this problem: "Why isn't a hamburger and a bottle of pop an adequate diet for me?" While the problem about diet seems to cry out for critical thinking and experimentation, let us take a good look at it.

What kinds of hypothesis-testing are possible? The one that first comes to mind is to carry on nutrition experiments with rats, guinea pigs, or hamsters. Ignoring the fact that the learner who is emotionally involved with pop and hamburgers will dismiss the results with, "They are lower animals, and this doesn't prove anything about humans," there is another problem. The results of such experimentation must be statistically valid. This requires a large number of experimental animals—a larger number than most schools can either afford or house. Unfortunately, we must reject this problem, although it is a real one, and retreat to the testimonial process.

Therefore, be selective. Not all problems can or should be solved through critical thinking. Keep thinking: "Is it worth the time, expense, and energy? Is it possible?"

BE ALERT

We sometimes pass over a real question that is the statement of a meaningful problem merely because it seems to be irrelevant at the time. If a learner asks, "Is cancer inherited?" or "Do we still believe in Manifest Destiny?", we are inclined either to answer the question, ignore it, or start a discussion on it immediately. The secret is to be aware that any question may be the beginning of a profitable exercise in critical thinking.

This is not to suggest that all lesson plans should be built around the concerns of the student—but rather to suggest that learners and teachers cooperate a little more. One cannot teach railroad trains to learners without first finding out about their problems relative to railroad trains. Perhaps the greatest problem for them is that they have never had a ride on one. Language arts, science, mathematics, and social studies at any grade level are such broad areas of study that one can surely take time to find out what the learners' questions and problems are.

Some of these problems may give you ideas and suggestions for future work or projects. It is indeed strange that some teachers will struggle through a unit or lesson in which no one is learning anything of any value, just because the course of study dictates this unit. Watch for questions that tell you of learner interest. If you do, you have started to overcome the problem of motivation or readiness. You have started the process of encouraging questions. As Yntema indicates, it is the great men of the world who are able to ask questions—almost anyone can answer questions.

BE HELPFUL

Let us suppose that a question of importance has been asked by the learners. This means that the problem for study has been stated. The next step is to isolate hypotheses and to begin to test them. It is here that the teacher must be helpful. Many times, of course, the teacher must be helpful in the setting up of problems and the formulation of conclusions, but the time when this helpfulness is most needed is in the steps of hypothesis-formation and testing.

Sometimes the learners will set up hypotheses that are impossible for one reason or another. The helpful teacher at this point will explain why they must be rejected. If there is a desire to test certain fabrics in the social-studies room, the teacher may have to veto some of the suggestions. For example, the test for silk may very well be too dangerous. If the learners in the English classroom want to test a hypothesis with an extended field trip, the teacher may have to veto it on the basis of cost. If the learners want to use an abacus to test a hypothesis in the mathematics class, the teacher might suggest buying rather than building, since to build an abacus would be too time-consuming. Once again, these activities were not worth the time, expense, and energy.

Sometimes being helpful involves helping the learners to sharpen their questions, hypotheses, and conclusions until they are real statements of problems, tentative solutions, and principles. However, often the best way in which to be helpful is to get out of the learners' way while they are thinking critically.

BE RESOURCEFUL

Learners will need help in setting up hypotheses tests that involve various kinds of resources. The resourceful teacher will know the fields of films, filmstrips, pamphlets, and all sorts of community aids. Other teachers in the building, businessmen downtown, and representatives from industry will be able to act as human resources, but the teacher must be resourceful in making suggestions to the learners regarding the use of these helps.

One of the best ways to find out about these resources is to check the yellow pages of your telephone directory.

None of these suggestions are made with the idea that all of the learners must see the same film, go on the same field trip, or, indeed, participate in any of the activities as a group. Perhaps only one learner—the one who is testing a hypothesis or forming a conclusion—need perform these activities. However, the resourceful teacher knows where to find aids when they are needed.

BE OBSERVANT

Imagine that the learner or learners have pursued the method of critical thinking to the point of formulating a conclusion. They have set up a problem, formed hypotheses, and tested these hypotheses. They have drawn a conclusion. The step that may very well be the most important part of the critical-thinking process is ready to be made. This step is one of behavior—the action based upon the conclusion that has been drawn. The observant teacher watches the learners to be sure that they act as if they had solved a problem through critical thinking.

For example, if the class has studied the effects of

microorganisms on the human body, the observant teacher makes sure that they wash the apples served at the midmorning lunch. If the class has studied literary criticism, the teacher watches to see what type of literature the learners select for their own enjoyment. If the class has studied intolerance in the classroom, the teacher is alert to expressions of social misinformation.

There is an obvious reason for the necessity for observation of learners. That is, a thing can be called "learned" only when it becomes a part of a behavior pattern. The learned principle must either change behavior or reinforce previous desirable behavior patterns. The ancillary reason for this observation is to communicate the idea that conclusions that were found through critical thinking are important enough for the teacher to be watching for evidence.

BE QUIET

Probably more scientific inquiry, or critical thinking, is stunted because the teacher talks too much than for any other reason. Many times teachers will say: "The answer to that question is . . . ," "That won't work," "You can't do that," etc. The best way to improve the learners' skill in critical thinking is to let him alone, always remembering that you must be selective, alert, helpful, resourceful, and observant.

When you have helped your learners become better in the skill of scientific inquiry, what have you done? You have helped them solve problems in a way that will enable them to resist propagandists, make intelligent choices, and generally become better citizens. Not that they will solve all problems this way—that would be inhuman. But we can hope that they will not vote for a man because he has a pretty smile, that they will not buy patent medicines and go to quack doctors.

Keep remembering that critical thinking is not limited to classroom studies. It applies to all areas of activity. Also remember that it is a skill, and thus must be practiced. No one was able to type, play the piano, draw a picture, or speak in a foreign language the first time he tried. Neither is anyone able to use the method of critical thinking without practice.

The Process of Critical Thinking

More often than not, the teacher-learner pursuit of the critical-thinking skill occurs in the verbal exchanges to be found in the classroom. With respect to these verbal exchanges, it might be pointed out that times have changed. Francis Hopkinson outlined a mock discussion in which a teacher attempted to force a student into the precise language that is so important a part of real critical thinking. The following was written in 1784:

TEACHER: What is a salt box?

STUDENT: It is a box made to contain salt.

TEACHER: How is it divided?

STUDENT: Into a salt box and a box of salt.

TEACHER: Very well! Show the distinction.

STUDENT: A salt box may be where there is no salt; but salt is absolutely necessary to the existence of a box of salt.

TEACHER: Are not salt boxes otherwise divided?

STUDENT: Yes—by a partition.

TEACHER: What is the use of this partition?

STUDENT: To separate the coarse salt from the fine.

TEACHER: How? Think a little.

STUDENT: To separate the fine salt from the coarse.

TEACHER: To be sure. It is to separate the fine from the coarse. But are not salt boxes yet otherwise distinguished?

STUDENT: Yes—into possible, probable, and positive.

TEACHER: Define these several kinds of salt boxes.

STUDENT: A possible salt box is a salt box yet unsold in the hands of the joiner.

TEACHER: Why so?

STUDENT: Because it hath never yet become a salt box in fact, having never had any salt in it; and it may possibly be applied to some other use.

TEACHER: Very true. For a salt box which never had, hath not now, and perhaps never may have, any salt in it, can only be termed a possible salt box. What is a probable salt box?

STUDENT: It is a salt box in the hand of one going to a shop to buy salt, and who hath sixpence in his pocket to pay the grocer; and a positive salt box is one which hath actually got salt in it.

TEACHER: Very good. But is there no instance of a positive salt box which hath no salt in it?

STUDENT: I know of none.

TEACHER: Yes, there is one mentioned by some authors. It is where a box hath by long use been so impregnated with salt, that although all the salt hath been long since emptied out, it may yet be called a salt box, with the same propriety that we say a salt herring, salt beef, etc.

There are several complaints that could be made here pedagogically, but lack of precision of language is not one of them. The teacher, of course, was discussing something of relatively little importance to the learner. The questions are all teacher-initiated. The verbal fencing goes on *ad nauseum*. There is, however, no question but that the teacher intends that the learner will use clear phrasing and accurate description.

This type of dialogue, if carried on in a modern school setting, might be similar to this:

TEACHER: Today I'm going to give you an unknown material and I want you to identify it without touching or smelling the sample.

(*The problem is originated by the teacher, but it is real and stimulating.*)

STUDENT: It's water.

(*This is hypothesis Number 1.*)

TEACHER: Lift it.

(*The teacher is initiating the testing of the hypothesis.*)

STUDENT: (*lifting the sample*) It looks like water, but it's awfully heavy.

STUDENT: (*inspecting the sample*) It's too heavy to be water.

(*This is a tentative rejection of the hypothesis.*)

STUDENT: I don't know any colorless liquids besides water.

(*Confusion here, but also a springboard for hypothesis Number 2.*)

STUDENT: What about alcohol?

STUDENT: I wouldn't know. What about it?

STUDENT: Alcohol is lighter than water. What other substances are there?

STUDENT: We can never find out by trial and error. Let's find some of its properties. We'll freeze some and boil some.

(*Here is an implied hypothesis Number 3 and a suggestion for the testing of further hypotheses.*)

(LATER)

STUDENT: It boils at 77° C., but we can't freeze it with ice. Do we have any dry ice?

(*In this step, data are accumulated.*)

TEACHER: Here.

(LATER)

STUDENT: It freezes at about −22° C. I'm still in the dark. Let's see if it will burn.

(*Here is more data plus further testing suggestions.*)

STUDENT: It might explode.

TEACHER: What if Karen is right? Get me a platinum wire. We'll try a little bit at a time.

(Here the teacher is obligated to try to avoid possible danger. He steps in to show a safe method of testing combustion properties.)

STUDENT: Should we use the hood?

TEACHER: Oh, yes.

STUDENT: It doesn't burn.

STUDENT: Let's find out how heavy it is.

(More information is sought.)

STUDENT: How?

STUDENT: Weigh a graduated cylinder then add 100 cc and weigh it again.

(Another testing technique is developed.)

(LATER)

STUDENT: It weighs 160 grams, so its density is 1.6 grams per ml., its melting point is $-22°$ C., and it boils at $77°$ C. But I still don't know what it could be.

(At this point a summary of data is probably advisable.)

STUDENT: Let's add some water to it.

STUDENT: The water floats on top.

STUDENT: Try alcohol.

STUDENT: It dissolved. What else can we do?

TEACHER: You've discovered many of the descriptive properties of the substance. Someone smell it.

(The teacher steps in to help straighten out the confusion.)

STUDENT: Whew! It's chloroform or something.

(This is the first tentative conclusion.)

STUDENT: We'll look in the chemistry handbook to see if chloroform has the properties we've discovered.

(A necessary check on the conclusion.)

STUDENT: It can't be chloroform. The freezing point is too high.

(A rejection of the conclusion.)

STUDENT: What is the formula for chloroform?

STUDENT: $CHCl_3$.

STUDENT: This might be fairly close. Chloroform isn't heavy enough. Can we replace the H with another Chlorine? What is CCl_4?

(*Another hypothesis is offered.*)

STUDENT: It is CCl_4. Everything checks. Fairly closely, anyway.

(*Here is the confirmation of the conclusion.*)

It should be noted that the teacher did not intrude upon this process unless it was absolutely necessary. That is, when a test became too dangerous, when clarification or motivation was necessary, or when a summary was important.

In the elementary grades the same techniques are possible:

TEACHER: How many pints of water in a quart of water?

STUDENT: Four pints.

STUDENT: Three pints.

STUDENT: Two pints.

TEACHER: We certainly are hearing a great many different answers, aren't we? Is anyone sure his answer is correct?

(*A pause is necessary here in order for the learners to realize that there can be but one possible answer.*)

TEACHER: Since no one is sure, how can we find out the answer for ourselves?

(*Here is an attempt to get the learners to think of tests for their hypotheses.*)

STUDENT: We don't know.

TEACHER: Sue, there are some bottles in the cupboard on the bottom shelf. Bring some of them over and place them on the table. Dave will help you.

(*The teacher prepares to give help in testing hypotheses.*)

STUDENT: I see how the bottles will help us find the answer.

(The dawn of an idea comes.)

TEACHER: How can they help us?

STUDENT: We can compare their sizes and see.

TEACHER: First, which of these bottles should we use to find the answer to our problem?

(The teacher is urging more precise definition of the hypothesis test.)

STUDENT: We'll have to use a pint bottle and a quart bottle.

TEACHER: Do you know which is a pint bottle?

STUDENT: The one in front must be, because it is smallest.

STUDENT: She's wrong, because that is only a half-pint bottle. This one is a pint bottle, because it says so on the bottom.

TEACHER: Bob, will you show the class where it tells you the size of the bottle? Let's put it over here by itself and find the other bottle. What size must this one be?

STUDENT: It's a quart bottle. I can see where it's marked.

TEACHER: Would you show it to the class? Now, what would be the next step in finding our answer?

STUDENT: We'd have to compare the sizes of the two bottles. You can see that the quart is two or three times as big as the pint bottle.

(Here is found another hypothesis.)

STUDENT: But we can't tell for sure how much bigger it is or how much more water it will hold unless we use some water, and then we won't have to guess at it.

(A test for the hypothesis is suggested.)

TEACHER: How should we go about it? What is it we are trying to find out?

(The teacher urges another statement of the problem.)

STUDENT: We are trying to find out how many pints of water there are in one quart of water. We will just fill the quart jar with pints of water. May I please be the one to keep score?

While the teacher in the elementary grades might intrude more often than the teacher in the secondary grades, it is still not necessary to supply too much information to the learners. More frequent clarification might be given, but the teacher still does not initiate too many suggestions.

The process of critical thinking can be used when we are dealing with only one learner, as in this example of a boy and his father:

BOY: Dad, why is that buoy out there painted black, and the one farther up the river painted red?

FATHER: Can you see any other difference in those buoys? (*The father refuses to answer the question directly.*)

BOY: One has a light and a bell, and the other just a bell.

FATHER: Is there a difference in their location?

BOY: The black one is on this side of the river, and the red one is on the other.

FATHER: What about the buoy on the other side of the island?

BOY: That buoy doesn't look like the other—it looks like a garbage can.

FATHER: They call that a "can" buoy. What else about it?

BOY: There are no lights.

FATHER: What else?

BOY: It's black and it's on this side of the channel.
(*The father is helping the boy narrow in on the statement of the problem.*)

FATHER: It better be.

BOY: There's another can buoy, but it's red. Maybe that's so the freighters can see it better.
(*The hypothesis is stated.*)

FATHER: What about all the red buoys we've seen?

BOY: They aren't the same size and shape.

FATHER: What about their location on the river?

BOY: They're all on the other side of the river.

FATHER: What about the black buoys?

BOY: They're all on this side.

FATHER: Why?

(The father is urging the formation of the hypothesis.)

BOY: It might be so that they don't hit the shore at night.
But all the freighters have to do is shine their spotlights to see the shore.

*(The boy states the hypothesis and tests and rejects it
himself.)*

FATHER: Is there a time when the spotlights won't do any
good?

BOY: When there is a heavy fog.

FATHER: In a fog, would it do any good to know what
color a buoy is?

BOY: If you knew that all the buoys on the American side
were black, and the ones on the Canadian side were
red, you would know what side of the river you
were looking at.

*(A confirmation of a hypothesis test is stated, and a con-
clusion is drawn.)*

FATHER: What good would that do? You still couldn't see.

BOY: You would know where you were going just by looking at your map.

FATHER: Right, son. There is a rule that says: "Red,
Right, Returning." That means that all the red
buoys will be on the right side when you are returning from the sea.

(The confirmation of the conclusion.)

In this case, skillful questioning, plus rational
thought were necessary. The confirmation of a conclusion such as this often comes from an authority figure,
however.

In the following example, we find an illustration of a lesson in which the learners explore the total process of critical thinking. Here, the problem has already been solved, but the learners need to examine what has happened and what they have done.

TEACHER: Do you remember discussing the stone that was brought into class and the sand bars along the lake, and how we came to some conclusions about these two things? I wonder if we could discuss the method we used to come to these conclusions?

STUDENT: We examined the facts and found what they told us.

TEACHER: We did something before this that was important. What was the first thing that we did?

STUDENT: The very first thing we did was to find what we wanted to draw conclusions about.

TEACHER: That's right. We had a problem we wanted solved. Then what?

STUDENT: Then we found out all we could about the stone and about meteorites, to see if what we had was a meteorite.

TEACHER: What did we do in the case of the sand bars?

STUDENT: We just looked at all the things that were different about the bars along the river and put them all together and arrived at a conclusion as to what made them different.

STUDENT: We had a problem to solve, we collected information about the problem, and we drew a conclusion.

TEACHER: Didn't we do a little more than that?

STUDENT: We had a conclusion about the stone when we started to find out what it was, and we had a conclusion about the sand bars before we looked up the wind direction.

TEACHER: Why did we continue if we were wanting to

arrive at conclusions when we had them already?

STUDENT: We wanted to make sure they were right.

STUDENT: Then we collected more information to see if we were right.

STUDENT: No, not exactly. We collected more information to see if the conclusion we reached fitted the new information we found.

TEACHER: Sort of a test for our hypothesis?

STUDENT: Yes.

TEACHER: Now, how did we arrive at the solution to our problems?

STUDENT: We defined our problem. Then we collected facts about the problem. We drew a conclusion about the problem. We tested the conclusion by seeing if it fitted other facts.

TEACHER: Do you think that this would work in other situations to solve other problems we have here in class?

STUDENT: Yes.

TEACHER: How about out of class? Might this method still work?

STUDENT: Yes.

TEACHER: Now, give me some examples where you have used such a method to solve a problem.

Of course, teaching for critical thinking is not always as simple as it might appear in these examples. Let us cite a case in which a teacher asked a group of twenty-six learners of third-grade level to answer on paper the following question: "What would happen to us if the sun were to disappear?"

There were only four answers that were given by more than half of the learners:

1. The earth would be dark.
2. No plants could live.
3. No animals could live.

4. There would be little heat.

As we might expect, the more abstract concepts, such as those concerning gravitational attraction, were not mentioned.

The problems confronted by the teacher in getting the youngsters to hypothesize seemed to be three in number. There was a lack of sophistication in seeing relationships. For example, many of the learners failed to see that the lack of much heat might well be the cause of a lack of evaporation, and they listed these as two separate phenomena.

Many of the learners failed to see that they were not answering the question that was asked. In these cases, the teacher received answers such as, "Something might happen to us" or "Something might go wrong on the earth." Neither of these represents a possible hypothesis.

Thirdly, many of the learners would restate a hypothesis two or three times in different words, not recognizing that they were repeating themselves. For example, one youngster said: "The earth would go dark. We would have no light. We couldn't see." These were listed as three separate hypotheses.

Frustrating as these results might have been to the teacher, the learners had made attempts to hypothesize. The refinement of this skill is the responsibility of the teacher.

Helping Learners to Identify Problems

There are basically only three typical occurrences in the classroom that may start learners on the road toward critical thinking. The first, initiatory happening is the question that is posed by the teacher. While some may say that this is the poorest way of helping learners to identify problems, others will, with justification, disagree. Of course, if the teacher identifies the problem in specific terms, part of the critical-thinking process has been done by the teacher. On the other hand, if the question is vague enough to be only a question, yet concrete enough to elicit some questioning by the students, the process is not impeded.

The second method of helping learners identify problems is to let the learners ask their own questions. This incidental method is quite effective in that it permits the learners to explore more meaningful problems than does the questioning of the teacher. It suffers from the disadvantage of being rather haphazard—rarely permitting an organized program in any curricular area.

The third method can be called the lucky accident. When something unusual occurs—a tornado, an election, an assembly program—perhaps it will bring with it an external stimulation to ask questions and formulate problems.

The examples given in the preceding chapter were all cases of critical-thinking initiation of the first type —the question that is posed by the teacher. The following vignette is of the second type—in which the learners ask the beginning questions.

STUDENT: Can't rust be prevented? Not even by painting the iron sheets?

(*The statement of the problem is made by the student.*)

TEACHER: Do new cars and other newly painted iron or steel surfaces rust?

(*The teacher is helping the student to refine his problem —that is, to find the subproblem.*)

STUDENT: No, not right away, but they often start to rust after a year or two.

TEACHER: What prevents rust during that first year?

STUDENT: New paint. Then, doesn't paint prevent rust, at least for a while?

(*Here is the refined statement of the problem.*)

STUDENT: How can we make it last longer?

(*Here is a refined statement of a subproblem.*)

STUDENT: You could put it on thicker or put it on every two years or so. Bridges and highway signs get painted every five years or so, to keep them from rusting away.

(*This statement is a combination of a hypothesis statement and a test of that hypothesis.*)

STUDENT: But they still get some rust. Can we invent a paint that will prevent iron from rusting for fifty years? You can't preserve iron for that long by putting paint on thicker, and even when you paint every two years, some rust still forms.

(*The hypothesis has been tentatively accepted, and another subproblem has been identified by a student.*)

STUDENT: Rust is a chemical change. You can't stop it. Iron just tends to get rusty. I don't think you can make a paint that will last a long time.

(*The hypothesis is rejected but without the use of verified data.*)

TEACHER: What is necessary for a chemical change to occur?

(*The teacher is questioning the previous statement, but it is done in a subtle manner.*)

STUDENT: Oxygen unites with the iron surface and forms into iron oxide. The iron itself changes when air can get to it.

STUDENT: If we could keep the air from getting to the iron, iron oxide could not form. Paint keeps the oxygen away from the iron.

TEACHER: Does this mean that we could find a rustproofing paint?

(*The teacher helps the class to return to the problem.*)

STUDENT: Yes, if we could find a paint that prevents the oxygen and iron from uniting in the form of rust.

(*A conclusion is reached.*)

The following example is a case of a lucky accident. The teacher had planned a field trip to one of the local parks, which not only had numerous flowers, trees, and shrubs, but also wildlife which was accessible for study purposes. As the group of learners passed a small pond where fish were kept, a tame Mallard duck landed on the water. While the learners were looking at him, he began to bob his head in and out of the water.

STUDENT: Shoo him away! He'll eat the fish.

(*Here is an unwarranted conclusion.*)

STUDENT: He isn't eating the fish.

(*A conclusion based upon data.*)

STUDENT: He may not have got one yet, but he sure is trying.

(*Another unwarranted conclusion.*)

STUDENT: He's not even interested in eating the fish.

STUDENT: Why won't the duck eat the fish?
   (*The problem is stated.*)
TEACHER: Let's sit down. Maybe we can answer this question.
STUDENT: They can't get them with their bills.
   (*The hypothesis is stated.*)
STUDENT: Why not?
STUDENT: He would need a long pointed bill.
   (*Here is an intellectual test of the hypothesis.*)
STUDENT: And look, he has a short, wide bill.
   (*Observational datum is given.*)
STUDENT: The pointed bill can be used to grasp wiggling fish.
   (*The hypothesis is presumed to be correct. Therefore, it is accepted as a conclusion.*)
STUDENT: What does he eat?
TEACHER: What could he eat, with a bill shaped like that?
   (*Another problem is stated, and the teacher asks for hypotheses.*)

In order to help learners identify problems, the teacher must keep several things in mind. To begin with, an assessment of the abilities of the learners relative to their skill in identifying problems must be made. The teacher must know whether the learners are able to sense problems that might be the start of the critical-thinking process. More than this, the various subproblems involved in the larger problems must be sensed. For example, while we all recognize "war" as a problem, we must be able to recognize the specific subproblems involved in this major problem. The teacher, therefore, must be insistent that the learners be able to state not only the major problem but also the subproblems. These statements usually take the form of questions.

A side issue in statements of problems is one of vocabulary. The learners may have trouble in phrasing their questions, and help must be given them.

In order to give practice in the formulation of problems, specific time must be given during the school day in which the learners are encouraged to raise problems and ask questions. These problem suggestions can be given during a general discussion period or in a more or less private interview with the learner. One very effective technique used by many teachers is to plan an overview lesson in which the important questions can be asked. This method permits a certain amount of necessary curriculum control by the teacher without stifling the questioning activities of the learners.

Helping Learners Formulate Hypotheses

In that phase of the critical-thinking process in which the learners must formulate hypotheses, the teacher can use one of two different techniques. In the first method, all of the various hypotheses can be listed, and then either tested one by one or each one may be investigated by a group of learners.

The second method is to test each hypothesis as it is mentioned. It may well be that this second method is inferior to the first in that if we test each hypothesis before we go to the next we will be making some unnecessary tests. That is, the teacher will find that after a list of hypotheses has been discussed before testing, several of these hypotheses can be rejected without ever being tested.

The following example is of the type in which several hypotheses are listed before testing begins.

STUDENT: Yesterday I went in our car past a big forest of trees with pails or tin cans hanging on them. What are those for?

(*The problem is identified.*)

TEACHER: Perhaps some of the others have seen this. Has anyone seen what Bob has just described? What are they?

(*The teacher calls for hypotheses.*)

STUDENT: I haven't seen them, but I guess the pails are full of water and they are used to feed the trees.

(*Here is hypothesis 1.*)

STUDENT: I've seen them and I bet I know what kind of trees they are. I saw a picture in a book of a rubber tree, and those pails are what has the rubber in them.

(Here is hypothesis 2.)

STUDENT: The pails might catch the bugs that crawl up and down the tree.

(Here is hypothesis 3.)

TEACHER: We have several suggestions about the answer to the question, but before we come to a conclusion we should have a little more information. What size were the trees?

(The teacher starts the learners in the process of collecting data.)

STUDENT: They looked big and they had lots of branches without leaves.

TEACHER: How were the pails attached?

STUDENT: There was a little wire thing sticking out of the tree and they were hanging on that.

STUDENT: Then my idea of using the pail to catch bugs wouldn't work. The pails would be too far out from the tree.

(Hypothesis 3 is rejected.)

STUDENT: I could get the encyclopedia and see if we could find pictures of different kinds of trees.

STUDENT: I could look for a picture of a rubber tree.

(Plans are made to explore hypothesis 2.)

STUDENT: Maybe my mother could take me back out there to ask the owner what's going on.

(A plan is suggested for testing all hypotheses at once.)

The following example illustrates the testing of each hypothesis as it is mentioned.

TEACHER: What else do we know about sound?

STUDENT: I heard something about a jet making so much noise that it broke some windows. Is that what you mean?

(The first tentative suggestion.)

TEACHER: We can add to our list that sound is a form of what?

(*The problem is stated.*)

STUDENT: Noise?

(*A hypothesis is given.*)

TEACHER: What must we have to do the work of breaking something?

STUDENT: Work is done by energy.

(*The hypothesis is tested.*)

TEACHER: So sound is a form of what?

STUDENT: Energy.

(*This is a conclusion.*)

TEACHER: What do I mean if I say that all sound is produced by vibration?

(*Another problem.*)

STUDENT: Something moves back and forth very fast.

(*A hypothesis.*)

TEACHER: Let's see if this idea is correct.

(*A testing is encouraged.*)

STUDENT: When we hit a drumhead and touch it, we can feel it vibrate.

In order to formulate hypotheses, it is necessary that the learners have at their disposal as wide a collection of sources of information as possible. This means that they must be taught to use reference materials, to take notes, to use reading aids, etc. The learners must also be taught how to interview resource people.

With regard to the statement of the hypothesis, the learners must be able to select relevant material from the vast pile of irrelevant material that they will find. They must be able to see relationships between two or more ideas, as well as the weaknesses and strengths that are to be found in data. Finally, the hypothesis, once arrived at, must be stated in the form of a generalization—a positive one rather than a negative one.

Helping Learners Test Hypotheses

Once the hypothesis has been stated, it must be tested. It can be tested either actively or passively. Some hypotheses lend themselves to active testing, others to passive testing. If, when planning a trip, we are confronted with two alternative highways that connect two cities, we must hypothesize that one road is the best road to take. To test this hypothesis, we compare mileages, check road conditions, etc. This is done passively. It would indeed be foolish to drive one road, then drive the other, in order to compare routes.

On the other hand, to hypothesize that one brand of automobile is better than another without actively testing this hypothesis would be equally foolish. After a hypothesis is formulated, a decision must be made relative to the efficiency and effectiveness of the active versus the passive method of testing hypotheses.

The following is an example of passive testing in which no attempt is made to establish the absolute validity of a hypothesis.

STUDENT: What's the best age to let people start voting? Some states let people vote when they are eighteen.
 (*The problem is stated.*)
STUDENT: Yes, I read in the paper that they do, but you can't always believe what papers and magazines say.
 (*A side issue is raised.*)
STUDENT: They wouldn't print anything unless they had a reason.

TEACHER: Is that the problem that we should be exploring at this particular time?

(*The teacher puts the class back on the right track.*)

STUDENT: No. The problem really is, "Is eighteen a better age to begin voting than twenty-one?"

(*A restatement of the problem.*)

STUDENT: Maybe some of the magazines and books have some articles in them. We could look in the library.

(*A hypothesis test is proposed.*)

TEACHER: Fine. Someone can review the current literature. How else can we find out?

STUDENT: I'll ask our lawyer. He'll tell us.

(*This student is reverting to the method of testimony.*)

TEACHER: Can't we reach our own decisions?

STUDENT: We could compare the articles and books we read. But how can we tell if they are right?

STUDENT: We have to decide about how accurate and truthful they are.

TEACHER: How?

The following is an example of the active testing of a hypothesis.

TEACHER: Why won't a candle burn if you put a snuffer over it?

(*The statement of the problem.*)

STUDENT: What does a snuffer do?

(*A subproblem.*)

STUDENT: It could either put out the flame by squashing it or it could just keep air away from the flame.

(*Two hypotheses are offered.*)

STUDENT: I don't think it would be squashing the flame alone, because I can put my finger right through the flame and the flame stays right where it was.

(*Rejection of one hypothesis.*)

STUDENT: Then I guess we would say the snuffer keeps air away from the flame.

STUDENT: That means a candle needs air to burn.

(*The hypothesis is refined.*)

STUDENT: We should set one candle in the air and see if it burns. Remember, we should have a control. We can put another candle in a jar and put the cap on. We should see some difference.

(*Active testing is suggested.*)

In order to test hypotheses, data must be accumulated. This means that the learners must have certain facilities at their disposal. These facilities include written materials as well as audiovisual aids and experimentation equipment.

Learners must be taught to arrange data in the form of tables, graphs, and charts. All kinds of summarizing techniques must be constructed and interpreted. The outline is an effective method.

Authorities of various kinds must be used in checking data, and decisions must be made relative to the expertness of these authorities. Finally, all tests of hypotheses should be checked.

Helping Learners Draw Conclusions

Although we generally think of a conclusion as a large generalization that is the solution to a problem, in fact this is not often true. Actually, a conclusion is most often a generalization of a great number of subsolutions to a great number of subproblems.

In this example, a conclusion is reached that is a solution to a problem of fact.

STUDENT: What are profits?
(*This is the problem.*)

TEACHER: Suppose you are in the worm business. You sell worms for fifty cents a dozen and you have four dozen worms to sell. How much would you take in?
(*The teacher proposes a subproblem.*)

STUDENT: I would take in two dollars if I sold them all.
(*A subsolution is offered.*)

TEACHER: What if your mother charged fifty cents to pay for the mess that the worms made in the house, and the food for the worms cost you one dollar and fifty cents?
(*Another subproblem.*)

STUDENT: There wouldn't be anything left for me to spend.
(*Another subsolution.*)

TEACHER: How do you feel about selling worms now?
(*Another subproblem.*)

STUDENT: If there isn't anything for me to spend after taking care of those worms all winter, I don't feel very good about it.
(*Another subsolution.*)

TEACHER: How can you arrange it so that there is some
left over for you to spend?
(*Another subproblem.*)

STUDENT: I don't think I can talk my mother out of her
fifty cents for the mess I made, and I would have
to pay for the food if I wanted to have the worms
live through the winter. I can raise the price of the
worms to seventy-five cents a dozen.
(*Another subsolution.*)

TEACHER: How would you come out then?
(*Another subproblem.*)

STUDENT: I would take in three dollars and only pay out
two. That would give me a dollar for myself.
(*Another subsolution.*)

TEACHER: That part that is left over is quite important.

STUDENT: I would rather have it than not.

TEACHER: What if you did a lot of work for an old lady
and received no payment?
(*Another subproblem.*)

STUDENT: I would feel that I had done somebody a good
turn.

TEACHER: Would that be a reward?

STUDENT: If I didn't get that feeling I wouldn't be very
happy about the job.
(*A subsolution.*)

TEACHER: Is that feeling something left over for you, like
when you sold the worms?

STUDENT: Profit must be something left over after you
have done something.
(*The conclusion.*)

In this example, a conclusion is reached that is a
solution to a problem of attitudes.

TEACHER: Let's talk about some of the reasons that Lassie
appears to be such a wonderful animal. Do you

think a dog can do all the things Lassie does every
week?

(*The teacher outlines the problem.*)

STUDENT: Most dogs haven't been trained or talked to
enough. Some people spoil their dogs.

(*A hypothesis is offered.*)

TEACHER: If one dog can be trained to do helpful things,
can't all dogs?

(*A subproblem.*)

STUDENT: No.

TEACHER: Can we say that Lassie can think?

(*Another subproblem.*)

STUDENT: We don't know if she saw a problem in the
first place. We don't know how many times she
tried to do what she did.

(*A hypothesis.*)

STUDENT: And a person watching another person or animal can't see thinking going on.

(*A test of the hypothesis.*)

STUDENT: It just looks true when we see Lassie doing
something. We don't know whether they are brib-
ing her when the camera isn't pointed at her. We
just can't assume anything about it.

(*The conclusion.*)

One of the most bothersome things to the teacher
is that too many human beings jump to conclusions.
This means that it is the responsibility of the teacher
to make sure that the learners formulate their conclusions on the basis of adequately tested hypotheses.

The conclusion should be an answer to the original
problem or question. Thus, it is stated as a declarative
sentence. If the original problem was one that was
real and meaningful to the learners, and if the steps of
critical thinking were taken in a sensible manner, it

would seem that the learners should apply their conclusions to new situations. In other words, they should behave in the future as though they had really solved a problem through critical thinking.

Further Uses of Critical Thinking

Learning facts and principles is not the only use to which the skill of critical thinking can be put. To begin with, the ability of the learner in using this method is a valuable factor in the evaluation procedure. We must remember, however, that we are to evaluate their abilities to identify problems, formulate hypotheses, test hypotheses, and draw conclusions just as carefully as we evaluate their abilities to memorize facts. More than this, none of us are in any position to state that one step of the critical-thinking process is more important than the others.

A learner who can draw conclusions but cannot formulate hypotheses is no better at critical thinking than one who can formulate hypotheses but cannot draw conclusions. The important ability is to apply the conclusion in a new situation.

In addition to the use of critical thinking in the area of evaluation, there are many other uses. The following is an example of the use of the method in the area of consumer education. In this case, the students had read a newspaper clipping concerning alleged government food-stamp irregularities. A loan company and a grocer had been accused of collusion.

STUDENT: The grocer received two dollars' worth of food stamps he didn't give anything for.

STUDENT: The recipient received two dollars less than the value of the stamps if they had been used at the store.

TEACHER: Let's try another comparison.

STUDENT: The recipient received two tenths, or one fifth, less for taking cash instead of goods.

STUDENT: Turn that around. The grocer received stamps for two tenths, or one fifth, more than the amount he paid the recipient.

TEACHER: What did the recipient really receive?

STUDENT: He received eight tenths, or four fifths, of the value of the stamps.

STUDENT: And the grocer received ten eighths, or one and one fourth, the amount he had paid for the stamps.

TEACHER: Can you think of anything else?

STUDENT: Yes, the loan company got its money by cheating people out of stamps they need for food.

STUDENT: Pretty low. They are cheapskates.

STUDENT: It's not fair.

STUDENT: When you deal with a loan company, they take your money when you go back to work.

STUDENT: Well, after all, you owe it to them.

STUDENT: It's probably automation that's causing all this crooked business.

STUDENT: Unemployed workers can take a training course to get a new job.

STUDENT: I still think they should do away with automation and give the jobs back to the people.

TEACHER: Wait a minute. First of all, can we give up all those new inventions? Don't they represent progress?

The following is an example of the use of critical thinking to combat prejudice.

STUDENT: I've always been interested in Eskimos and the way they live. Boy! I wouldn't want to live in Alaska. All they ever have is ice and snow and igloos to live in.

STUDENT: Why did we accept them as the forty-ninth

state? I imagine that only a few of those Eskimos can read and write.

STUDENT: I don't think that all of Alaska is the same. I knew a man who was there during the war, and he said that parts of Alaska are just as modern as anyplace in the world, and the weather isn't too bad, either.

STUDENT: Well, what is Alaska really like?

TEACHER: It certainly looks as if everybody has a different idea about what Alaska is really like. Our study of this state should be quite interesting. Suppose we look at some of the ideas that you have mentioned.

The following is an example of the use of critical thinking to improve critical abilities. The teacher had been role-playing.

STUDENT: Aren't we going to have a chance to set up part of the program for today?

TEACHER: No. I'm afraid not. I've decided that you haven't been learning as much as you should, so I'm going to have to do all the planning. Well, what seems to be the trouble? Everyone looks rather disappointed.

STUDENT: We'd like to go back to the way things were.

TEACHER: What do you mean, the way things were?

STUDENT: Before, we had a chance to say what we thought we needed to do in part of the day, but now you do all of it.

TEACHER: You mean that I have been doing all the legislating?

STUDENT: Have you been doing this on purpose?

TEACHER: Doing what on purpose?

STUDENT: Not giving us a chance to work together like we used to.

STUDENT: He's been trying to show us how an undemocratic classroom would be run.

TEACHER: What do you mean by "undemocratic"?

STUDENT: When some of the people don't get a chance to
   express their opinions.

TEACHER: That sounds pretty familiar.

STUDENT: Some of us looked at our lists of rules of democracy, and we think that in the past two days you
   have broken all of them.

TEACHER: You mean that I am guilty of breaking all
   the rules?

STUDENT: Yes. When you break one of the rules the others
   fall apart.

TEACHER: Can you give an example?

STUDENT: Well, when you decided to do all the planning,
   that meant we couldn't vote, and the majority and
   minorities had nothing to say, and we couldn't make
   our own plans anymore.

TEACHER: That sounds reasonable.

The following is an example of the use of critical
thinking to explore a completely unknown area.

STUDENT: Billy put some crayons on the steampipes and
   they are melting all over the floor.

TEACHER: What a mess! Why did you do that?

STUDENT: I wanted to see if they would melt.

TEACHER: What made you think they might melt?

STUDENT: Crayons are like candles. Say, isn't that a pretty
   color? I wish we had some paint this color.

TEACHER: First of all, you must remember that this mess
   is yours to clean up. But you do have an idea. Can
   we use this melted crayon in some way?

STUDENT: Why couldn't we paint with it? It would get
   hard again like crayon.

STUDENT: But see how thick it is—would that work? It
   would just stick to the paint brushes.

STUDENT: Can't we use something else besides paint brushes?

STUDENT: We could paint with sticks, and just sort of "dab" the melted crayon on. We might even be able to make things look rough with it.

STUDENT: Or after the crayon was on, we could use the side of the stick to smooth it out.

TEACHER: I think your ideas are fine. But we have a problem. Billy's method of melting the crayon isn't very practical. How can we melt crayons without making a mess?

STUDENT: We could put crayons in a pan and melt them on a stove.

STUDENT: We don't have a stove.

STUDENT: How about putting the crayons in a baby-food jar and putting them on the steampipe?

The following is an example of the use of critical thinking in group guidance.

TEACHER: Sue, what are your plans?

STUDENT: My parents want me to finish high school and go on to college. But I'm not sure what I want to do. Instead of wasting their money and my time, I guess I'll go to work after high school.

TEACHER: Why do you think it's a waste of time and money to go to college?

STUDENT: I'm only speaking for myself, but I think that most girls go to college to find a man to marry. I think I can do that just as well without going to college.

TEACHER: Is that the only reason?

STUDENT: No. There are others. The main one is that there doesn't seem to be any need for a girl to go on with her education after high school unless she is very smart. What can she do even if she does graduate? She still ends up married and a plain housewife.

There doesn't seem to be a need or a place for educated women in America today. What can she do
besides becoming a secretary or nurse or something
like that?

STUDENT: What's wrong with being a nurse?

STUDENT: There are more opportunities today for women
than ever before, and in all fields, too. Things are
opening up as far as jobs for women go. Look at
the women in Russia.

STUDENT: And as for her argument about women getting
married and having children—so what? You can still
work after your children are old enough to go to
school. Besides, what's wrong with being an educated housewife? Maybe your family will be better
off because you are educated.

STUDENT: If a woman is married to a man who went to
college, she will have a better chance of making
him happy if she is educated. She may be a better
mother, too.

TEACHER: You have raised some good points that we need
to consider.

The following is an example of the use of critical
thinking in creative expression. This playlet was written by the learners. The setting is a rocket ship nearing
the moon.

ARNIE: Frank, what do you think it's going to be like up
there?

FRANK: I've heard many stories about the moon being
made of cheese.

ARNIE: I don't believe it, but I'll keep my eyes open, just
in case.

FRANK: There it is! Just think, we are the first men to reach
the moon, you and I.

ARNIE: I guess we had better gather our equipment and
prepare for a landing, huh?

FRANK: Yes. Wait! We seem to have run into a bit of trouble.

ARNIE: What's the matter?

FRANK: The instruments all show a tremendous rise in temperature. It's too hot to permit a safe landing.

ARNIE: I'll bet it's really true about one side of the moon being very hot and the other side very cold. I don't know about you, but I'd rather land on the cold side.

FRANK: Maybe we had better land on a spot just between the cold and the hot side—in the twilight zone. We'll have to watch the instruments.

ARNIE: The folks back home will be pretty excited to hear about this.

FRANK: Mother will be proud.

ARNIE: What do the instruments register now?

FRANK: It's safe to land.

ARNIE: Prepare for landing.

FRANK. All set. Look at the camera! I dropped it and look at it bounce! We remembered weights for ourselves, but forgot them for our instruments. They weren't kidding when they said that the gravity on the moon is less than that on the earth. I just couldn't imagine things being able to bounce so much higher on the moon than on the earth.

ARNIE: Look at those mountains.

FRANK: They're so high.

ARNIE: Let's take a closer look.

FRANK: Arnie, do you see what I see?

ARNIE: Where?

FRANK: Right in front of you.

ARNIE: Holy mackerel! It's a crater.

FRANK: I wonder how deep it is.

ARNIE: Miles and miles, I bet.

The following is an example of the use of critical thinking in combating ignorance.

STUDENT: What's fluoride?

TEACHER: How did you happen to hear about fluoride?

STUDENT: I saw it on television, and they said that some toothpaste had fluoride in it.

STUDENT: It does. And the people who use it have fewer fillings in their teeth.

STUDENT: Does fluoride keep your teeth from getting rotten?

STUDENT: How come if I've had fluoride treatments and it's so good, I still have to go to the dentist?

STUDENT: I remember my dentist said that everyone should have their teeth checked regularly.

STUDENT: What are fluoride treatments?

TEACHER: Can someone describe them?

STUDENT: *I* can. I had them last year. They put this fluoride stuff on your teeth and it doesn't hurt a bit and it's supposed to help your teeth get strong.

STUDENT: How come they do this if you can get fluoride from toothpaste?

TEACHER: There are many ways you can get fluoride. Some ways may be better than others.

STUDENT: I read in a magazine that the best way for fluoride to work is to have it in your water so you get it all the time, and if this is true, how come we don't have it in our water? They have it in the water where my aunt lives.

TEACHER: Putting fluoride in the water is called "fluoridation," and this has been a very important issue in our town. Some people want it and some don't.

STUDENT: How come some don't want it?

STUDENT: My mother says it makes your bones weak.

STUDENT: I heard a man say it was against his religion.

STUDENT: My neighbor says it makes your teeth get spotted.

STUDENT: My mother also said it would cost a lot of money to have it put in our water.

TEACHER: These are many of the arguments against

fluoridation, but don't you think we need to know a lot more about it to understand it more clearly?

STUDENT: We shouldn't believe everything we hear, should we?

TEACHER: That's very true. We should know and understand something before we form opinions about it.

STUDENT: If some say it's bad and some say it's good, how can we decide what it is?

TEACHER: Don't you think that if we are able to learn more about it we might be able to make our own decisions? Where do you suppose we might get some information?

STUDENT: I'll go to the library and look.

STUDENT: Do you think the County Health Center might have some information on it?

STUDENT: Do you suppose we could have a dentist come and talk to us? I can ask our neighbor. He's a dentist.

TEACHER: These are all fine ideas. Let's get to work.

There is really no limit to the uses of the critical-thinking process in the classroom. Surely we owe it to the learners to help them solve problems in an intelligent manner. This is a skill that they will always need.

Index